Contracting for Project Management

CONTRACTING FOR PROJECT MANAGEMENT

Edited by
J. Rodney Turner

GOWER

Published by
Gower Publishing Limited
Gower House
Croft Road
Aldershot
Hampshire GU11 3HR
England

Gower Publishing Company
Suite 420
101 Cherry Street
Burlington, VT 05401–4405 USA

British Library Cataloguing in Publication Data
Contracting for project management
   1. Project management 2. Contracting out
   I. Turner, Rodney
   658.4'04

Library of Congress Cataloging-in-Publication Data
Contracting for project management / edited by J. Rodney Turner.
     p. cm.
   "This book is derived from the Gower handbook of project management, 3rd edition"–Pref.
   Includes bibliographical references.
   ISBN 0–566–08529–1 (pbk. : alk. paper)
   1. Contracting out. 2. Letting of contracts. 3. Project management. I. Turner, J. Rodney
(John Rodney), 1953– II. Gower handbook of project management.

   HD2365.C66 2003
   658.7'23–dc21

                                                                                    2002035444

ISBN 0 566 08529 1

Typeset in Century Old Style by Bournemouth Colour Press, Parkstone and printed in Great Britain by MPG Books Ltd, Bodmin, Cornwall.

Contents

List of figures

Notes on contributors

THE EDITOR

Rodney Turner is Professor of Project Management in the Department of Marketing and Organization of the Faculty of Economics, Erasmus University, Rotterdam, and a director of EuroProjex, the European Centre for Project Excellence. He is also a visiting professor at Henley Management College and adjunct professor at the University of Technology, Sydney. After leaving Oxford University, where he completed his doctorate and was a post-doctoral research fellow at Brasenose College, he spent several years with ICI working on engineering design, construction and maintenance projects in the petrochemical industry. He worked as a consultant in project management with Coopers and Lybrand before joining Henley Management College. He has been with Erasmus University since 1997. Professor Turner works as a project management consultant. He lectures worldwide, and has published several books and papers on project management, including the best-selling *Handbook of Project-based Management*. Rodney Turner edits the *International Journal of Project Management*, is Vice-President and past Chairman of the Association for Project Management, and immediate past Chairman of the International Project Management Association.
rodneyturner@europrojex.com

THE AUTHORS

Peter Baily is a Fellow of the CIPS. He has been a consultant and a contributor to courses and conferences in several European countries, in Singapore and in the USA. He became the first full-time lecturer in purchasing in Britain at about the time his book *Purchasing and Supply Chain Management* was first published. This was the first comprehensive treatment of the subject to appear in the UK, or indeed anywhere outside the USA. He is also co-author of *Purchasing Principles and Management*, a standard textbook on the subject.

Denise Bower is a lecturer in construction project management in the School of Civil Engineering, Leeds University. She is also a consultant for the Oriel Group Practice and Indeco, internationally recognized project management consultancies. Her recent work includes the evaluation of procurement and corporate strategies, the development of partnering guidelines, the evaluation of success criteria for partnering arrangements, and recommendations of contract strategies for overseas projects. Denise's research interest is the optimization of the procurement of contracted services. She is a member of the Post-Latham Working Group 12, which produced the guide *Partnering in the Team*. She is the author or co-author of many books and publications, including *Engineering Project Management, Dispute Resolution for Infrastructure Projects* and *Managing Risk in Construction*. d.a.bower@leeds.ac.uk

Peter Marsh is principal of Peter Marsh Associates, contract consultants. He qualified as a solicitor, and has an honours degree in management sciences. He was chief contracts officer at the National Coal Board, before becoming central contracts manager for GEC. He later joined STC as manager of contracts administration, subsequently becoming projects manager for its Submarine Cable Division. Peter then held a number of senior appointments in the George Wimpey Group, which included commercial director of British Smelter Construction, director of business development for George Wimpey International, and a director of Wimpey Major Projects. He is the author of *Contract Negotiation Handbook* and *Contracting for Engineering and Construction*, both published by Gower.

Stephen Simister is a director of Oxford Management & Research Ltd, a project management consultancy specializing in assisting clients to scope and define project requirements to meet their business needs. He has experience of most business sectors and has been involved in all stages of project life cycles. Previously, Stephen worked for Bovis Program Management, an international construction consultancy. He is a fellow of the Association for Project Management, and is chairman of the Contracts & Procurement Specific Interest Group. He is also a chartered building surveyor with the Royal Institution of Chartered Surveyors and sits on the construction procurement panel. Stephen has a doctorate in project management from the University of Reading with which

he maintains close links. He lectures and undertakes research contracts at a number of academic institutions including Oxford University, London School of Economics, UMIST, and Henley Management College. He has published widely in the field of project management, risk and value management. He is joint editor of Gower's *Handbook of Project Management*.
s.j.simister@omr.co.uk

Fotis Skountzos graduated from the National Technical University of Athens in 1992, with an MEng in mining and metallurgical engineering and then worked on the Athens Olympic Metro, being responsible for construction of a large diameter tunnel. He then took an MSc in engineering project management at UMIST and graduated in 1998, after writing his dissertation on partnering. Since then he has worked as a project manager for ADK SA, consulting engineers in Athens.
fotchrys@otenet.gr

Nigel Smith is professor and head of the Construction Project Management Group in the School of Civil Engineering, University of Leeds. Nigel has obtained funding for research projects valued at over £750 000, undertaken in collaboration with industrial partners. As a project director of the European Construction Institute he has headed a DETR-funded research project into the use of incentive contracts. He has been organizer, chair or co-chair of conferences in Florence, Budapest, Trondheim, Moscow and Bonn. Nigel has published widely, with 14 books and over 80 refcreed papers to his credit.
n.j.smith@leeds.ac.uk

Preface

A project is a temporary organization to which the owners assign resources to achieve their development objectives. For anything but the smallest projects, the owner will not have sufficient resources in-house, and so will need to procure additional resources from outside. Thus contracting is an essential part of project management. It is the way the project owner brings in additional resources to create the project organization. This book provides an introduction to project contract management.

There is a theme underlying the book, expressed in Chapter 3, that in creating the project organization, the owner should want all the resources to be motivated to achieve the objectives. In order to do this, the owners should create a contracting environment which encourages a cooperative organization, and aligns the contractors' objectives with theirs. They should not create a conflict organization, in which the contractors have a completely different set of objectives. Unfortunately, project owners so often aim for the latter under the misguided view that it will give them a better outcome, whereas all they create is a lose–lose outcome.

This book is derived from the *Gower Handbook of Project Management*, 3rd edition, edited by me and Dr Stephen Simister. It contains the chapters from Part F, on project contract management. To those chapters, I have added one more, written by me, on selecting farsighted contract forms to achieve a cooperative project organization. The book aims to provide an introduction to project contract management for project managers. The first four chapters describe forms of contract. The remaining five chapters are each on a separate topic. There is a chapter giving an overview of contract law, followed by a chapter on partnering, benchmarking and incentive contracts. The next chapter describes how the owner procures contracts and materials. This is followed by a chapter written from the perspective of the contractors, describing how they should bid for work. Finally, there is a chapter on variations, claims and disputes.

The book is written by several authors. There is a small amount of overlap between chapters. The authors may also give different perspectives of the same topic. Never do we contradict one another, but different views can provide a broader understanding of the subject.

Chapter 1: Roles and responsibilities in project contract management

In Chapter 1, Nigel Smith describes the roles various parties can fulfil on a project, especially the managerial roles. He then describes how different types of contract attempt to define these roles, and deals with the relationship that arises between the clients, their contractors and subcontractors. He covers the traditional procurement route first, client–engineer–construction contractor, and uses this as a basis to compare others against. The traditional route has been the basis of contracting for centuries, and it is therefore inevitable that other routes will be variations on that theme. Nigel then describes some of the other more modern, but now common, approaches. There are integrative approaches, which give the contractor responsibility for more steps of the life cycle, particularly integrating detail design and construction, and there are managerial approaches, which give the contractor greater management responsibility. Finally, he considers some of the emergent routes now being used. He also describes the terms and conditions for the employment of project managers.

Chapter 2: Contracts and payment structures

In Chapter 2, Peter Marsh describes the other dimension of contract forms, the different methods of pricing contracts. These include fixed price, cost plus and remeasurement contracts. He then considers how the contract price is set, and how progress is measured and payments made as the project progresses. He starts with an overview of the contract forms as described by Nigel Smith, and includes a section on the factors to be considered when choosing contract forms.

Chapter 3: Farsighted project contract management

In Chapter 3, I derive a methodology for choosing contract forms. I start with the premise that the aim of project contract management should be to build a cooperative project organization in which the contractors are motivated to achieve the owner's objectives. The contract needs to be set up in a way that properly motivates the contractor. It also needs to be farsighted and flexible enough to deal with unforeseen circumstances as they arise. I then describe two schemas from the transaction cost literature. One measures the ability of a contract form to incentivize and appropriately reward the contract, taking account of the risk. The other measures its ability to provide farsighted, flexible governance. I go on to describe modern practice in choosing different contract forms, and use that to derive a methodology. I show that the appropriate form depends in the first instance on who controls the risk, the owner, the contractor, or both together. It then depends on whether the risk is on the project's product or method of delivery, and the overall complexity of the project.

Chapter 4: Standard forms of contract

Parties to a contract can draw up a bespoke contract document at the start of every project. However, that is both inefficient and subject to error. Better to use standard forms of contract, which are tried and tested, based on expert knowledge and readily available. Almost every industry has standard forms of contract, especially the three branches of the construction industry. In Chapter 4, Steve Simister and I describe the use of standard forms, and give a listing of some of those available.

Chapter 5: Contract law

In Chapter 5, Peter Marsh gives an overview of contract law. His coverage is primarily based on English law, but most of the elements of English contract law are common in other legal systems. He describes the elements of contract formation, including offer, acceptance and consideration. He then considers conditions of invalidity, including mistake, misrepresentation, duress and frustration. Finally, he describes the terms of the contract called conditions and warranty. These include issues such as the price of the contract and payment, quality and performance, guarantees and exclusions, the passing of property and risk, delivery, completion and possible damages in the event of breach.

Chapter 6: Partnering, benchmarking and incentive contracts

In Chapter 6, Denise Bower and Fotis Skountzos describe partnering. These types of contract are becoming increasing popular and aim to remove the adversarial culture that has built up in the construction industry. They define partnering and describe its key elements. They then consider its benefits to both parties and barriers to its successful achievement. In the construction industry, benchmarking can be a key element of multi-contract partnering arrangements, as clients and contractors try to improve performance on projects from one contract to the next. They give an overview of benchmarking in construction and how it relates to partnering arrangements. Finally, they describe how incentives can be built into partnering contracts.

Chapter 7: Procurement

There now follow two chapters about how the client and contractor go about entering into a contract. In the first, Chapter 7, Peter Baily describes project procurement. He considers the special characteristics of project purchasing and the role of the project purchasing manager. He then describes the procurement of contracts and subcontracts, and the purchasing of goods and equipment. There are two short sections on the amendment of purchase orders and electronic data interchange.

Chapter 8: Bidding

Contract management is often written from the client's perspective. In Chapter 8, Steve Simister addresses that balance. He describes how a contracting organization should bid for work. There are three stages in the bid process: before receiving the invitation to tender, bid preparation and submission, and contract negotiation. He covers each in turn.

Chapter 9: Managing variations, claims and disputes

The main purpose of the contract is to describe how the relationship will work. However, it would be dangerously complacent to assume it will work perfectly every time. It is therefore necessary to deal with situations where it will be less than perfect. In most cases, the changes to the contract will be relatively small and they can be dealt with simply. It is even possible to deal with quite large changes within the structures of most contracts. However, in the worst cases there is disagreement about the extent of the change, or who is responsible. That may lead to a more extensive claim and, if either party disagrees about the claim, possibly to a dispute. In Chapter 9, Peter Marsh describes variations, claims and disputes.

1 Roles and responsibilities in project contract management

Nigel Smith

No organization has all the skills required to do anything but the most simple of projects. Additional skills required for the completion of projects must be bought in from external sources. In this chapter, we consider the roles required throughout the project supply chain, particularly during the design and construction stages, and what contract types are available to provide the additional roles in different ways. The contract is the mechanism by which:

- the project organization is created;
- project managers arc employed;
- goods and services are procured;
- the commercial nature of the project process is defined.

It is important for project managers to be aware of how to operate effectively using the contractual procedures to optimal advantage. This chapter reviews the roles of different parties to a project and different contracting practices designed to provide the client organization with those services. It covers the traditional approach and some of the more recent but now common practices, as well as emerging ones. The chapter also describes standard terms for project managers and comments on future trends.

PROJECT PROCUREMENT

Ideas for projects arise from many sources, including strategic planning, market forecasts, process re-engineering or suggestion by a speculative developer. A client considers the viability of these concepts to determine the extent to which it wishes to participate. This varies from client to client and project to project, from being a wholly internal, private project executed by direct labour to a public sector concession awarded to an external promoter. Whatever delivery structure

1

is adopted, similar functions need to be undertaken, many of which must be sourced from outside the client's organization. The roles and responsibilities for the management of a project can be viewed as a hierarchical sequence of interlinked functions (Figure 1.1). These cascade down from the strategic, market and commercial drivers acting on the client and progress through the various parties in the entire supply chain. Due to the range of types of procurement strategies used in projects, this generic diagram may use separate titles for groups which in practice might be a single organization or even a single individual. Further, the rationale for the linkages included in the diagram would have to be modified to remain compatible with the structure and numbers of parties involved in the project.

One of the most important decisions to be taken after the client is satisfied with the project concept and viability is the choice of procurement strategy. This has to identify the number of parties involved and their responsibilities. This is not always straightforward and it is important to remember there are always alternative procurement routes available for any project. A number of differing sources estimate that the selection of the most effective procurement strategy compared with possible strategies could produce cost savings of about 8 per cent. This is significant when it is remembered that profit margins in construction are frequently of the order of 1–2 per cent.

In this chapter, we consider a number of different procurement strategies available to fulfil the roles illustrated in Figure 1.1. We start by considering the traditional approach, and then describe others as variants on this model. Ultimately, it is the client who must determine the procurement strategy to its optimal advantage.

THE TRADITIONAL PROJECT CONTRACT STRATEGY

As a starting point for the consideration of the roles and responsibilities of parties to a project suitable for all types of business, engineering or industry, we consider the traditional structure used extensively in the UK construction industry. This involves three parties:

- A client who initiates and sanctions a project.
- A consultant who undertakes the feasibility and design.
- A contractor who is responsible for implementing the project.

Procurement strategies adopted by a project must recognize the prevailing culture and structure of the indigenous construction industry, as these will have a major influence on the effectiveness of any strategy adopted. In the UK

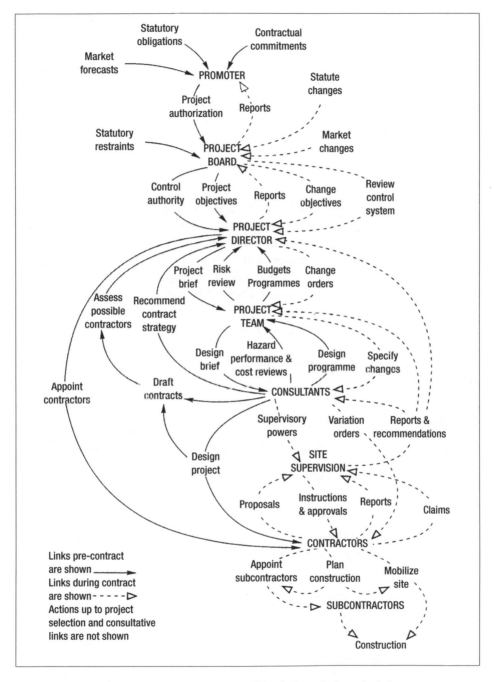

Figure 1.1   Roles and responsibilities in the project supply chain
Source: After Nunos and Wearne (1984)

construction industry, it has long been common practice to combine many of the roles in Figure 1.1 into the three fundamental roles listed above. Although not as popular as it was 20 years ago, this traditional procurement strategy still accounts for more than 50 per cent of all heavy civil engineering construction in the UK. It is also the basis for the Institution of Civil Engineers standard forms of contract, of which the seventh edition is the most recent version (1999). This strategy will therefore be outlined as a template against which other procurement strategies can be evaluated.

THE CLIENT

In the traditional procurement strategy, the client is the organization which desires the project, often owns the site, usually funds the project and is frequently the end-user. (Often in property development the client is the developer, the eventual owner a financial institution and the end-user an organization that rents the building.) It is also assumed that the client organization will contain the project board and the project manager who will have the authority and expertise to commence the procurement of the design and construction phases of the project. From Figure 1.1, it can be seen that this equates to the internalization of the roles and links associated with Promoter, Project Board, Project Director and Project Team. Nevertheless these functions remain and have to be undertaken effectively.

THE CONSULTANT

Consultants or consulting engineers are charged with three main functions:

- Management of the design process.
- Assistance in tendering and contract administration.
- Site supervision.

Typically, a design brief or scope of works is prepared by the client organization and consultants are selected on the basis of the quality of service provision and fee competition. The successful consultant will then have direct contact with the client.

Changes are now occurring to improve the working of the traditional system. For some time, the ICE *Conditions of Contract* (1999) has been the most widely used model form of contract in the UK. This is despite its being based on the assumption that the consultant as well as being paid by the client is also the independent arbiter of the contract. However, in 1995 the ICE issued the *Engineering and Construction Contract*, which recognized for the first time the

4

roles of 'designer', 'project manager' and 'site supervisor' as 'client agent' roles, with their duties and responsibilities defined accordingly. The role of independent arbiter is replaced by an external 'adjudicator', whose fees are paid equally by client and contractor (see Chapter 9). This was a major component of the Latham Report (1994). As we shall see, this new contract can apply to almost the complete range of procurement strategies and several clients are considering it as a direct replacement for contracts used in the traditional procurement strategy.

THE MAIN CONTRACTOR

Traditionally, a single main contractor would be appointed, usually after the completion of the design, to undertake construction only. The contractor would have responsibilities for planning the works, mobilization, construction and opening or commissioning. However, the traditional procurement system contains some inherent characteristics that adversely affect and restrict the effective construction of the works. First, by precluding the contractor from the earliest stages of a project, the opportunity to incorporate construction expertise at an early and cost-effective stage is wasted and subsequent changes enforced by requirements of practicability are often costly. Second, the client and consultant may have been working on the project for many months or, on large projects, for a number of years. But at tender stage a contractor is given between eight and ten weeks to understand the project, to liaise with members of the supply chain, to assess the risk and to produce a tender price. This tender price has to be high enough to protect the contractor from the consequences of risks for which it has responsibility, but low enough to be successful in a competitive tendering system based on the lowest evaluated price being successful. Third, there is often pressure from the client for the contractor to commence work on site at the earliest possible opportunity. This is usually a false economy as a short period of pre-construction planning time can often result in substantial time and cost savings on site. These savings can often be shared in some way with the client.

SUBCONTRACTORS

In the simplest form of contract, the main contractor may undertake the complete contract. However, it is common practice to make use of specialist subcontractors to undertake sections of the works. The subcontractor will have specific knowledge and expertise, with appropriately trained staff, which enables it to undertake specialist work more competitively than the main contractors. With or without subcontractors, there will also be a supply chain of varying complexity consisting of vendors, suppliers and service providers.

THE PROJECT MANAGER

So where in the traditional procurement system is the project management expertise? It is common for many organizations to 'manage by projects' and to employ key personnel as project managers. Indeed the client, the consultant, the contractor and the subcontractor may all have project managers. However, in terms of the complete project, it is the client's project manager that is considered to have responsibility for all the phases of a project and to execute the project management function. At some level inside the client organization, possibly the Board of Directors, a decision has to be made to authorize the project and to determine the terms of reference of the project manager. Terms are discussed in greater detail later in this chapter.

THE PROCUREMENT PROCESS

One of the first actions of the project manager, after determining viability and degree of risk, is to determine the project objectives. In all projects the primary targets, time, cost and performance are important. However, it is likely that one will be dominant. There are a host of secondary and tertiary targets which need to be considered. Typically the degree of involvement of the client and/or the project manager, the innovation required, interfaces with external organizations, inclusion of international organizations and many other factors need to be considered to establish the clear aims of the project. Only if the project purpose and objectives can be clearly defined can the most appropriate procurement strategy be identified. However, events might occur that require modifications or changes to the project objectives, and constant monitoring is necessary. This cycle is illustrated in Figure 1.1 between the Project Board and Project Director.

The project manager then has to consider his or her own internal project team and the other main parties, the consultant and contractor. The project team conduct risk analyses and investment appraisal, undertake feasibility studies, develop the project brief and determine the procurement strategy. For each contract the project manager considers the project objectives in terms of the combined selection of an organizational structure, a contract type, a tendering strategy and a model form of contract. In the traditional procurement strategy the consultants are appointed on the basis of a project design brief and competitive tendering. The project team and the consultant will interact during the design process and in the preparation of construction contract documentation. After completion or substantial completion of the design, the contractor is appointed on the basis of a priced bill of quantities and competitive price. It is usual for the project team to have undertaken a prequalification exercise prior to tender. This is popular with both clients and contractors. Clients favour prequalification because it removes financially or technologically weak organizations and ensures a large competitive 'pool' of contractors, each of which is appointable. It is also popular with contractors because prequalification removes organizations without the necessary skills, experience and management expertise and allows them to compete with peer group members who will have similar costs and overheads. Interestingly enough the appointment of a subcontractor is more likely to be based on negotiation of the price with the organization identified as being the 'best partner' than on open competition.

As mentioned above, other parties involved in the project may have their own internal staff with the job title project manager. Their role is to act as the point of contact between the client's project manager and the organization's own staff and to manage their own component of the project to meet their predetermined targets and objectives. It is therefore an important part of the project team's brief to try to harmonize the goals of these other project managers with those of the client's project manager and of the project as far as is practicable.

For the rest of this chapter it is the role of the client's project manager, or the organization undertaking that role, which will form the basis for discussion, thereby providing a view through the whole project life cycle. The client's project manager has responsibilities, some of which are contractual and others non-contractual. Model forms of contract differ in their structure and in the allocation of risks and obligations. Consequently, the client's project manager could find most of the contractual roles imposed from a contract of engagement or employment and might not have a direct contractual role in the contract between client and contractor, as in the ICE seventh edition *Conditions of Contract* (1999). Alternatively, the client's project manager could have a main contract role with specific obligations and duties, as discussed earlier in regard to the ICE new engineering document conditions of contract (1995).

ALTERNATIVE PROJECT CONTRACT STRATEGIES

Other established procurement strategies exist in construction and in other sectors and disciplines, but all of these can be examined by comparison with the traditional system. For the purposes of this chapter two main types of procurement strategies will be discussed, integrated strategies and management strategies, but within each type there are a large number of variants.

INTEGRATED STRATEGIES

As the name suggests, the essence of this type of strategy is to integrate roles and responsibilities for phases of the project. In particular the design, engineering and construction phases are integrated, removing the interface which in practice is often a cause of dispute and conflict. Hence, the client, by giving a single organization responsibility for both phases, transfers the management of interface problems and any associated risks. However, this is offset by the client losing control over a major part of the project life cycle.

If the project life cycle, as shown in Figure 1.2, is studied, it is clear that the design and construction phases of the project coincide with the maximum capital investment and thus the roles and responsibilities of the parties at this stage are significant. Although there is a plethora of integrated procurement strategies, they can be considered under three subcategories which reflect the extent of the project life cycle for which a single organization takes responsibility. From interrogation of Figure 1.2, we can identify subcategories, 'design and build', 'turnkey' and 'concession', with responsibilities ranging from part of design and construction phases to almost the whole project cycle.

Design and build

The simplest of the three, the design and build strategy, requires the client, often with a consultant, to complete the usual front-end activities, but instead of appointing a contractor on the basis of a completed design, only an outline design or a design brief would have been prepared. The design and build contractor would then be responsible for the detailed design and the engineering or construction and the management of that interface. These contracts tend to be used for relatively straightforward work, where no significant risk or change is anticipated and when the client is able to specify precisely what is required. Usually but not always the contractor is paid on a fixed price, lump sum basis to provide an incentive for the contractor to be cost-effective and to limit the client's investment.

Turnkey

Turnkey contracts as the name suggests are contracts where the client, on completion, turns a key in the door and everything is working to full operating standards. Consequently, turnkey contractors have responsibility for the design, construction and commissioning phases of a project. Frequently this will also involve the procurement of all main items of plant and equipment. Under this strategy the client's project manager usually prepares a performance specification

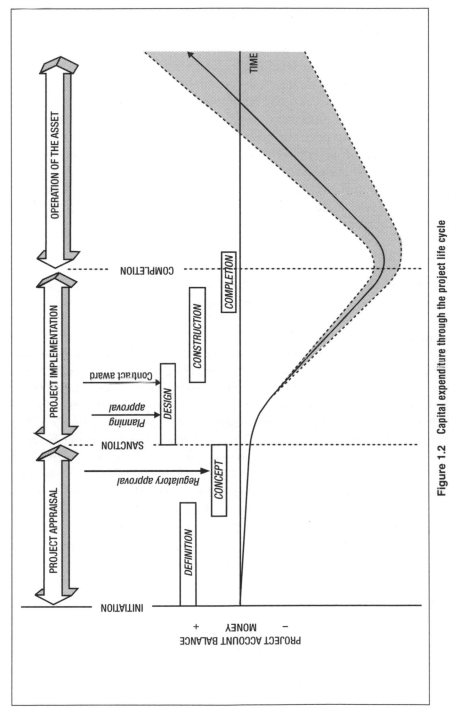

Figure 1.2 Capital expenditure through the project life cycle

The cumulative effect of several variable factors is to give a spectrum of uncertainty (shaded area) about the best prediction

Source: After Smith (1996)

and a scope document which determine the performance and the location and design constraints respectively. Due to the increased responsibility the cost of tendering is also increased and hence smaller numbers of bidders are invited. Typically selection is based on the evaluation of a two-package tender submission. Each bidder prepares a technical package containing process design, engineering design, procurement routes, erection and construction schedules and resources, certification and approval and commissioning procedures, and a financial package indicating the lump sum price and such breakdown as is required by the client. Once the contract has been placed the client role is severely limited and the client's ability to make any changes other than a formal contract variation is almost non-existent. The turnkey contractor's project manager has much greater multidisciplinary responsibilities and has to coordinate along the supply chain and across a series of project phase interfaces.

Concession

The transfer of almost the entire project is the possibility considered under the concession or Finance–Build–Own–Operate–Transfer (FBOOT) strategy (Smith 1996). This approach was encouraged by the UK government in the early 1990s under the Private Finance Initiative and in the late 1990s under the Public Private Partnership Programme. This subcategory covers almost all of the project life cycle including operation and maintenance, and the functions, roles and responsibilities of most of the parties identified in Figure 1.1 are integrated into a single organization, usually known as the promoter. The promoter is often a single project joint venture of minimal asset value formed solely for the purpose of undertaking the project. The other principal difference with this type of strategy is that the promoter has to arrange the project financing and generate a revenue stream sufficient to service the debt, operate the facility and provide an adequate return. In this case, the roles and responsibilities of the client's project manager are also transferred to the promoter's project manager but with the additional complexities caused by the promoter not being a single organization. The implications for the project manager are considerable and the effect of working within collaborative structures is investigated in greater detail later in the chapter.

MANAGEMENT STRATEGIES

The key element in this group is the additional emphasis placed on management of the project. The underlying principle is that additional management expertise can be provided to the client and hence provide benefits in terms of fitness for purpose, buildability, performance and risk management that will more than offset the cost of the expertise. This additional management resource is provided to the client when it is required and removed on completion without affecting the number of permanent staff in the client's organization.

As shown in Figure 1.3, the parties operate in a different manner, with the management contractor appearing as a separate entity and working closely with the client's staff and the client's project manager in particular. The management contractor would be appointed at a very early stage in the project. The type of organization operating in this role in the UK could be a consultant but is usually a contractor who would be experienced in the type of work and would otherwise be a likely tender bidder. In the role of management contractor a small team drawn from the contracting organization's staff would be selected and engaged usually on the basis of fee reimbursement plus profit margin. Naturally, to avoid possible conflicts of interest, the organization is then excluded from tendering for any of the works contracts. The management contractor works extremely closely with the client's project manager, almost like additional client staff and it would therefore be counter-productive to place harsh or onerous performance terms on the management contractor.

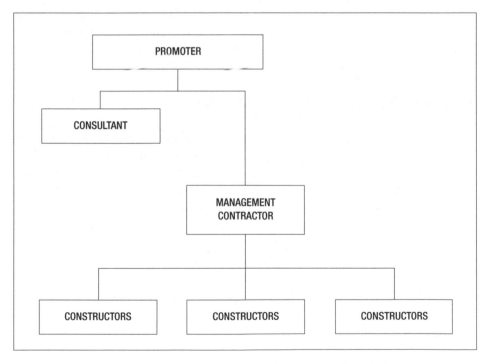

Figure 1.3 Organization structure of a management contract
Source: After Smith (1996)

The other parties have slightly modified roles also. The consultant is now engaged by the management contractor and will liaise on buildability and practical issues of design throughout the contract. The other different feature clearly shown in Figure 1.3 is that the use of a single main contractor has been replaced by a series of work package contracts. The management contractor selects and manages these contracts, and solves any interface problems which may arise between them. Each contract could vary, with some lump sum fixed price and some cost reimbursable, dependent upon risk and time constraints. By packaging the work into such small components, the contracts can be used to give greater client flexibility to overlap sections of the work and to assist with risk management. Hence to be effective the contract must produce benefits to the project manager in terms of access, flexibility to make change and effective management of construction which are less than the cost of engaging the management contractor team.

Each work package contract is managed by the management contractor in conjunction with the client's project manager on behalf of the client. Consequently, the client has no privity of contract, that is no direct contractual relationship with the consultant or works contractors, which places much greater importance on the relationship between the client's project manager and the management contractor. It is important that there is a degree of trust and common commitment if the contract is to be undertaken to reach its maximum potential benefit.

EMERGING PROJECT CONTRACT STRATEGIES

During the 1990s, there was a clear trend away from adversarial contracting strategies towards collaborative working, which has direct implications for the role and responsibilities of the project manager. In any type of collaborative working, there is a need to align goals, so incentives are often used, and there is a need for new agreements and contracts and a greater requirement for good management practice. Chapter 6 deals with the different types of collaborative working in detail, and Chapter 3 describes the adoption, incentivization and governance structures under different forms of contract to create a cooperative project organization. The present chapter will concentrate on the implications of these different organizational and contractual combinations from the viewpoint of the project manager.

JOINT VENTURES AND PARTNERING

The industry has been accustomed to the use of both horizontal and vertical joint ventures (JVs) and consortia for many years. More recently other forms have become apparent, including the various forms of partnering, such as alliancing, term partnering, project specific partnering, and forms of collaborative ventures to form promoter groups for Private Finance Initiative (PFI) projects. To operate these forms of procurement requires a culture change within organizations and, more importantly, requires new project management skills to deal with a range of new roles and responsibilities.

PUBLIC PRIVATE PARTNERSHIP (PPP)

Public private partnerships (PPPs) are a separate class of organizations which operate in a variety of ways but share the obvious common feature of having both public and private sector funding. Many projects which are politically desirable, in other words that have a higher social cost–benefit analysis than their financial analysis, cannot be funded by private finance on commercial terms. Their viability is ensured by the public sector reducing project risk to an acceptable level. The use of direct public debt financing is used very much as a last resort and risk sharing, concessions for existing revenue generating facilities and the provision of indirect benefits like tax holidays are more likely to be adopted. Nevertheless, if there is public sector involvement the public sector will want to be included in the project management process. Working within these hybrid organizations, the project manager is confronted by the culture clash between the two types of organizations and yet still has to make effective project decisions.

DISPUTE RESOLUTION

Disputes and more importantly dispute resolution are key issues in any collaborative agreement (see Chapter 9). Increasingly, the project manager is involved in finding equitable, speedy and cheap methods of resolving disputes and maintaining focus on the project. If disputes are left for any length of time, they can affect trust and commitment to the project, and the long-term stability of the collaborative agreement could be at stake. At the most extreme levels, parties might leave and need to be replaced, an option which should have been foreseen and allowed for by the negotiation of an agreement which allows for equitable withdrawal as well as equitable entry. However, the vast majority of disputes do not fall into that category and are often suitable for alternative dispute resolution (ADR) procedures.

ADR has been adopted in most countries around the world. It can be simplified as a series of six steps (Figure 1.4). The lower two steps, 'prevention' and 'negotiation', are present in all model forms of contract and are a core part of the traditional roles and responsibilities. Similarly, the final two steps, 'arbitration' and

Steps	Cost/Hostility	Name	Process
1	Low	Prevention	Risk allocation, Incentives for cooperation, Partnering
2		Negotiation	Direct negotiations, Step negotiations
3		Independent Expert	Dispute review board, Standing arbitrator or Independent expert
4		Mediation	Non-binding resolution, Mini-trial, Advisory opinion, Advisory arbitration
5		Arbitration	Binding resolution
6	High	Litigation	Civil Court, Judge, Jury

Figure 1.4   Dispute resolution steps

Source: After Dispute Avoidance and Resolution Task Force (DART) Report

'litigation', are also available to most contracts, although sometimes they can only be used on completion of the contract and tend to be lengthy and expensive. It is the middle two steps which as compulsory procedures form the basis for ADR, namely 'independent expert' and 'mediation'. Any dispute which cannot be satisfactorily resolved by negotiation, goes to the independent expert. This person, agreed upon before the start of the contract, is provided with both sides of a dispute, usually within specific and fairly limited time periods. The expert then responds within another fixed period of time with an expert opinion of the issues. This is purely an expert view, it is not legally constituted, it is not binding and it need not be equitable, but it does give the parties to the dispute a view of how the matter is likely to be viewed by others. This is sufficient sometimes for one party to accept another view on a dispute. However, if the expert's view does not result in any resolution, then the next step is mediation. A trained mediator, who ideally is not a lawyer, is agreed by both parties and his or her fees are paid jointly by the parties. A mediator tries to establish a middle ground position which is less than either side really wants, but hopefully is close enough to convince the parties to settle with no real winners or losers. Again, this is not mandatory, but the parties are aware that unless a settlement is reached at this stage the next stage will involve legal representation, will be time-consuming and will be expensive.

THE PROJECT MANAGER

Although the role of project manager is similar in any collaborative venture, the longer the duration of the collaborative agreement the more difficult it becomes for the project manager to resolve the dichotomy of working with long-established but time-limited partners. In one sense, the role is facilitated by increased knowledge, understanding, trust and commitment but complicated by the finite nature of relations and the commercial imperatives of possible future competitive strengths.

SPLITTING THE ROLES OF THE ENGINEER

The Institution of Civil Engineers produced a new model form of contract, *The Engineering and Construction Contract* (ECC 1995), which recognized the trend towards collaborative working and highlighted the need for good project management. One of the main features of this contract is the replacement of the previously pivotal role of the engineer with a set of client's agent roles, namely 'designer', 'supervisor' and 'project manager', and with the new role of adjudicator, an external role supported equally by payments from client and contractor. On small projects the three client's agent roles might be undertaken by a single person but normally this form of contract is giving clear cognizance to the three complementary roles which were formerly imposed on the engineer.

This contract is to be commended as a valuable attempt to clarify this difficult area of the roles and responsibilities of the project manager for construction contracts. The more traditional contract does not formally identify a project manager role and the precise nature of responsibilities is variable from organization to organization and from project to project. The ECC has provided a degree of certainty and common understanding for this complex problem.

STANDARD TERMS FOR PROJECT MANAGERS

Despite the relative longevity of the role and function of the project manager, progress has been very slow on the development of model forms of engagement. To date project managers have been employed using standard contracts for service providers, consultants and others, modified for the purpose, or bespoke forms of contract. Naturally the terms recommend appointing only qualified project managers and it is expected that they will be appointed in the earliest stages of the project.

In the UK in 1998, the Association for Project Management (APM) developed a set of standard terms for the appointment of a project manager (APM 1998). As with any model form, these terms are applicable to any project, in any location at any time and are drafted under English law. Needless to say, there is a mechanism for incorporating relevant specific project data; in this case, it is known as the schedule of particulars. Like all model forms, these terms will bring benefits in understanding, ease of use and common documentation if they become widely established.

The flexibility and applicability of the standard terms is further increased by having a permanent set of core terms and the choice of one from a number of sector specific schedules of services. One of the first tasks of the contract is to provide precise definitions of terms. In this document the 'client' is identified as the project manager's employer. The schedule of services will contain a listing and the client and the other stakeholders will decide what is to be added or deleted from the schedule to suit the particular project under consideration.

Payment is always a key issue. The terms contain a fee schedule for payment to the project manager on the basis of fixed prices, time-related charges and/or reimbursement of expenses. The issue of incentives is important, particularly as many projects are undertaken on an incentive basis. Should the project manager be paid at a professional rate with no variation or should a related incentive be linked to either the main contract or client satisfaction? Should even part of the fee be at risk if the project manager fails to perform? At present these options are not included in the standard terms, but could be added if required.

FUTURE TRENDS

In the UK, the construction industry has been relatively slow to innovate despite the advantages of improvements in other sectors and the general advances in establishing the discipline of project management. The introduction of the Construction Design and Management Regulations, the Latham Report (1994) and more recently the Egan Construction Task Force Report (1998) has indicated a move towards a more project-focused, collaborative system of working and sharing best practice and world-class performance.

Managing by projects is now becoming accepted across all sectors of industry. Even service provider organizations are moving towards the mechanism of internal and external projects as the basis for strategic development, managing change and adopting best practice. The emphasis given to the 'front-end' activities by project management has enhanced its appeal to general business in addition to the more traditionally project-based sectors. This spread of project management is likely to continue. It is interesting to note that European bankers publicized the 'project' to introduce the Euro, a term which would not have been used a few years ago.

It is always difficult to predict the future, but in essence this is what project management is about. Hence to foresee the future of project management itself is even more of a challenge. However, a number of issues stand out. Business in general is moving towards operating the concept of sustainability. This has implications for the wider contractual environment and the role of the public, or society, in projects. Equally people are increasingly concerned about environmental and community issues and the temporary and permanent effects caused by the implementation and subsequent operation of projects. The roles and responsibilities of project managers are likely to be widened to incorporate these additional demands. Indeed, until any project, in any location, at any date can be guaranteed to be completed on time, within budget and to the specified quality there will always be a need for project managers.

REFERENCES AND FURTHER READING

Association for Project Management (1998), *Standard Terms for the Appointment of a Project Manager*, APM, High Wycombe.

Egan, J. (1998), *Rethinking Construction*, Construction Task Force Report, London.

Institution of Civil Engineers (1995), *The Engineering and Construction Contract*, 2nd edition, Thomas Telford, London.

Institution of Civil Engineers (1999), *Conditions of Contract: Measurement Version*, 7th edition, Thomas Telford, London.

Latham, Sir Michael (1994), *Constructing the Team: Final Report of the Government/Industry Review of Procurement and Contractual Arrangements in the UK Construction Industry*, The Stationery Office, London.

Nunos, G. E. and Wearne, S. H. (1984), *Responsibilities for Project Control during Construction*, School of Technological Management, University of Bradford.

Smith, N. J. (ed.) (1996), *Engineering Project Management*, Blackwell Scientific, Oxford.

Turner, J. R. (1995), *The Commercial Project Manager*, McGraw-Hill, London.

2 Contracts and payment structures

Peter Marsh

The nature of the contract between the purchaser and the contractor can take one of a variety of forms. The nature of the contract depends on a range of issues, including the scope of the work, the responsibility of the contractor, the risk involved and the urgency. In this chapter we consider the types of contract structures adopted, different pricing regimes and the terms of payments. We also describe the issues to be considered when selecting the different options.

CONTRACT STRUCTURES

When choosing to use contractors, the purchaser may follow one of several procurement routes, distinguished by the following features:

- Whether responsibility for the design, procurement, construction and commissioning is placed with one organization, or is to be divided between several, separate organizations.
- Whether the main contractor will both manage the project and undertake construction, or will be responsible for the management only with the construction work undertaken by others, working either as subcontractors to the main contractor or as separate contractors employed directly by the client.
- The basis upon which payment is to be made.

There are several procurement routes commonly in use:

1. *The traditional system* Used in building and civil engineering contracts where the design responsibility is primarily that of the architect or engineer employed by the client and the contractor or contractors are primarily responsible for construction only. Some design work may be undertaken by specialist subcontractors nominated by the client, but this can raise difficult

questions of design responsibility. The client through their architect or engineer retains control of design during construction and of the general management of the contract. When required, they will issue variation orders. A variant of this may be for the appointment by the client of a project manager to provide management services and for the architect or engineer's functions to be limited to design.

2. *The turnkey contract*   This is where a single firm is employed by the client to undertake the design, procurement, construction and commissioning of the entire works, including managing the process. The client is only responsible for the preparation of their statement of requirements which becomes the strict responsibility of the contractor to deliver. This type of contract is used mainly for the design and construction of process plants and for projects financed using non-recourse financing such as one done under the Private Finance Initiative (PFI). The client does not retain an engineer in the traditional sense during construction and the client's functions are limited to those of inspection, payment and ensuring that the works meet their performance guarantees. This type of arrangement is sometimes called Engineering, Procurement and Construction (EPC).

3. *The design and build contract*   Equivalent to 2. above, in the building and civil engineering industry. Here, the contractor is responsible for design as well as construction. The contractor's detailed design is often developed from a conceptual design prepared by the client's designers prior to tender and the client's design team are often seconded to work for the contractor after contract award. The client will, however, retain an engineer to protect their interests.

4. *Construction management and management contracting*   Similar to 3. above, in that the contractor is responsible only for the management of the contract, with all construction work done by others. The distinction is that in construction management the subcontractors engaged to do the work are contractually responsible directly to the client while managed by the construction manager, whereas in management contracting they are employed by the management contractor as subcontractors. Design is often the responsibility of the client through the architect or engineer but the design process is managed by the contractor. Sometimes design is also made the responsibility of the contractor.

5. *Guaranteed maximum price*   Combines construction management with design and build. In outline this is typically as follows. The contractor is initially responsible for the management of the design phase of the contract including programming, coordinating the work of designers, including specialist firms, and tendering for the various packages of work. At a point

where a substantial portion of the contract has been tendered for, the contractor agrees a guaranteed maximum price with the client. The contract form for this second phase as well as the contractor's fee for overheads and profit will have been agreed at the time of the contractor's appointment for the first phase.

The appropriate method for a particular project depends on a number of factors including the following:

1. *The method of financing*   If the project is financed by non-recourse financing, that is the project itself provides the security for the loans, the banks are almost certain to insist on a turnkey route so the entire design is the responsibility of the contractor and the client's only responsibility is the preparation of their statement of requirements.
2. *The need to ensure the earliest feasible date of completion*   The quickest method is construction management with the contractor responsible at least for the management of design. This allows design and construction to proceed in parallel. It does not, however, provide the client at the outset with a firm price.
3. *The need to ensure the lowest initial capital cost*   This is most likely to be achieved using the traditional method although there is a risk that the consultant's design may not be the most economic since it will not have been tendered in competition. On the other hand, a contractor's design might not take account of the lifetime costs. There is also the risk of variations and claims which can cause the out-turn cost substantially to exceed the initial estimate.
4. *Certainty of the out-turn costs*   This is most likely to be achieved through the use of the turnkey method which is why it is favoured by the banks. Of course, this will only be so if it is feasible for the contractor to provide a total lump sum for the contract, which means that they must be able to obtain the complete information necessary for a firm lump sum tender. Also all the information must be available at the required time. This may increase the time required for tendering. It also means that the client must not change their mind later.

THE CONTRACT PRICE

There are three main ways in which the contract price may be expressed or calculated:

1. Lump sum.
2. Remeasurement, schedule of rates or bill of quantities.
3. Cost reimbursement.

On a single contract the different ways may be combined. On a building contract, the above-ground element of a building may be on a lump sum basis while the foundations are done on an approximate bill of quantities subject to remeasurement. The supply portion of a chemical plant may be done on a lump sum, while the installation of the plant is on cost reimbursement, but with the contractor's overheads and profit compounded as a lump sum.

The work package approach is a variant of the lump sum method. It is suggested as one of the main options in the *Engineering and Construction Contract* (ECC 1995) where it is called a priced contract with an activity schedule. The contractor prepares a list of all the activities which they expect to carry out in undertaking the work, and each activity is priced as a lump sum.

The choice of which way to price the work depends largely on the amount of information the purchaser can provide the contractor at the time of tendering, the conditions under which the work will be carried out, and thus the risk which it is sensible to expect the contractor to accept. A further factor will be the manner in which it is proposed to finance the project. If non-recourse financing is to be adopted, then almost certainly the banks will wish to see the project contracted for on a turnkey lump sum basis.

LUMP SUM

From the purchaser's viewpoint, and that of any financier, the ideal is a firm lump sum with the minimum provisions for variations or claims. It establishes the amount of the commitment in advance, it provides the maximum incentive to the contractor to complete the work on time and it reduces to a minimum the amount of administration involved after the contract has been let. However, these benefits will be obtained only if it has been possible for the contractor to tender realistically. It follows from this that in addition to the general information required by a tenderer, they must be able to assess the following from information provided by the purchaser, their own engineering staff or prior experience of similar work:

1. The ground conditions on the site.
2. Material quantities and specifications. Labour hours and trades both for shop production and on site. This will mean that method statements must have been produced.
3. Descriptions and quantities of bought-out items. This requires decisions to have been taken, for example, on sizes and capacities.

4. Types of constructional plant which will be required and for what periods.
5. The time required by the various categories of design staff involved.
6. The site organization and facilities which will be required and for how long.
7. Factors which will affect site productivity.
8. Geographical and climatic factors as they affect site work.
9. Access to site.
10. Local availability of materials and labour.

For work which is to be subcontracted, the firm must provide similar information to all the subcontractors to enable them to make a similar assessment.

The above is a formidable list. It confirms the need for the purchaser to give complete and accurate information before a lump sum price can be produced. It also indicates that for a major project, considerable time and cost will be expended in the preparation of the tender for a lump sum contract. What must be remembered is that every time a tenderer guesses, it may guess wrong, and if the tenderer is successful in obtaining the contract every wrong guess costs someone money. Moreover, if the contractor is to remain in business in the long run, that someone can only be the purchaser whether on that contract or another.

Just as the contractor's problem on lump sum tendering is to assess the risks involved, so the purchaser's problem is the time it takes for the information to be gathered and processed to reduce those risks to reasonable proportions. Some element of risk will always remain; that is the very nature of contracting. The problem of obtaining information in time arises particularly on contracts which involve work below ground, such as foundations for a structure, tunnelling or sinking of shafts. The drilling of extensive boreholes and examining the results takes time which management is frequently not prepared to accept. Even then there is no certainty that the conditions encountered below ground will be as predicted.

BILL OF QUANTITIES

A distinction must be drawn between two ways in which the term 'bill of quantities' is used.

In standard forms of building contract, where quantities form part of the contract, the contract price is a lump sum, not for the building as a whole, but for the stated quantities of work described in the bills of quantity. These quantities are an accurate estimation of the work to be performed by the contractor except where any quantity is stated to be approximate. If greater quantities of work are necessary to complete the works, then the contractor is entitled to be paid extra under the variations clause in the contract. The value of work in addition to the stated sum, or for which only an approximate quantity was given in the bills, is determined by measurement and is priced at rates given in the bills. Thus, although the contract starts as a lump sum it is the client who essentially bears the risk that the quantities are not an accurate estimation of the work, although the contractor takes the risk of an error in pricing. However, under the JCT standard form of building contract (JCT 1980) there are also a number of provisions under which the contractor is entitled to be paid an additional loss and expense, which will be discussed further under claims (see Chapter 9).

In civil engineering contracts, by contrast, the bills of quantity are only an approximate estimate of the quantities of work to be performed and, unlike a building contract, do not define the work for which a lump sum price is quoted. In a civil engineering contract there is no lump sum price quoted in the standard form of tender and it is stated in the ICE standard conditions 1999 that the price is to be determined by measurement of the work done. The valuation of that work is then made in accordance with the rates given in the bill of quantities, unless, for any item, the difference between the actual quantity and the bill quantity is such that in the opinion of the engineer the bill rate is unreasonable or inapplicable. There is no necessity in this case for the change to have been the result of a variation. It is assumed that the contractor's rates and prices for the work as stated under the contract are correct and sufficient. Thus for a change of rate to be accepted, the change in quantity must be such as to require a change in the method of working requiring different plant or organization or be so excessive as to completely change the scope of work. An example was the case of *Mitsui* v. *A.G. of Hong Kong* where the billed quantity of the most expensive tunnel lining was 275 m and the actual 2448 m (*sic*). The billed quantity to be left unlined was 1885 m and the actual 547 m. The billed quantity of steel required for lining was 40 tonnes; the actual was 2943. Not surprisingly, the contractor claimed the engineer had the power to adjust the rates in the contract. More surprisingly, the Hong Kong government claimed it had no such power. The Privy Council decided in favour of the contractor. As they pointed out, if the government were right there was a large element of wagering inherent in the contract.

In both building and civil engineering forms the contractor when pricing has to estimate the quantity and cost of the materials, labour, supervision and plant which will be required to execute the work. Since the largest elements are usually labour and plant, the assessment of productivity is a vital part of the estimating process. This in turn is closely related to:

● the physical conditions under which the work will be carried out, due, for example, to the time of year;
● the possibility of carrying out the work in a planned way with a reasonable

degree of continuity, due, for example, to drawings arriving on site well in advance of the scheduled commencement date of construction.

These points are referred to again when discussing variations and claims in Chapter 9.

COST REIMBURSEMENT

On some projects, where the facility delivered will earn substantial revenue, finishing by the earliest possible date is regarded as more important than obtaining the lowest capital cost. Yet the extent of the lack of definition of the project or the anticipated risks are such that it is impractical to expect the contractor to assume the risks of even a measurement and value contract of the type just discussed. In these circumstances, the only alternative is some form of cost reimbursement.

The obvious problem is that paying the contractor the actual costs of carrying out the work provides no incentive for the contractor to minimize the costs. Indeed many contractors do not like cost reimbursement because of the inefficiencies which it can breed within their own organizations. Therefore, various types of incentive or target cost contracts have been devised as a means of combining the flexibility and speed associated with cost reimbursement with a measure of financial discipline and an incentive to achieve economy and efficiency. All these forms of contract have certain features in common:

1. The principle of design and construction being conducted in parallel rather than in series.
2. The tendering by the contractor of a target cost either as a series of lump sums for the carrying out of defined packages of work or for a bill of quantities.
3. The tendering by the contractor of its fee inclusive of profit and overheads.
4. The recording of the actual costs incurred by the contractor which should exclude any costs associated with defective work or re-work to remedy defects.
5. At the end of the contract the making of a comparison between the target and the actual costs. For this purpose, the target must be adjusted to reflect any variations or other events for which the contractor is allowed compensation under the terms of the contract.
6. The sharing between the purchaser and the contractor of the difference between the adjusted target and the actual costs in proportions set out in the contract.

Where the forms of reimbursement contract differ is in their treatment of the contractor's management fee. The Engineering and Construction management form (ICE 1995) provides for this to be a percentage of the actual cost and to be included within the comparison between target and actual cost. In other forms the contractor's fee is a lump sum and is not made part of the comparison. Where the management fee is to be a lump sum, the most careful definition is needed of the items to be included in the target cost and those to be included in the management fee. For example, it may be advantageous for the purchaser to include within the management fee if it is to be a lump sum elements such as the costs of the procurement of materials and of the site management staff and facilities. As to the percentage sharing arrangements between the contractor and the employer, various alternatives are available, but it is suggested that these arrangements should be kept as simple as possible and that it is recognized that there are two objectives:

● To provide the contractor with a genuine incentive to complete the work for a cost below the target.
● To protect the purchaser from the worst effects of a substantial cost overrun.

If time is particularly important, it is possible to build in an additional incentive by varying the share of the savings accruing to the contractor according to whether or not the contract is completed early or late. This may be done as shown in Figure 2.1.

There are many problems with target cost contracts:

1. There is the setting of the target itself. The intention must be that the target is realistic and is not to be either beaten or exceeded by significant amounts. It should not be far outside the normal limits of estimating accuracy. However, the target cost form of contract has been chosen because the uncertainties and risks involved in the contract do not allow the tendering of a lump sum price.

2. Because of the risks and uncertainties, including those arising from the lack of design definition, there is a real chance of substantial variations being required during the course of the contract. The effect of variations on the actual cost will be picked up automatically, in that the contractor is to be paid the actual costs of doing the work. However, it is also necessary for the target cost to be adjusted to take account of the variations. While this may be easier if the target costs are contained in comprehensive bills of quantity, the rates may well not be applicable to the change which has occurred, especially if it is of a design nature. Nor is the use of bills of quantity applicable to all types of contracts.

3. The use of a target cost contract imposes a substantial administrative and

Early/late completion (weeks)	Contractor's share of savings (%)
–6	90
–4	75
–2	60
0	50
2	35
4	20
6	nil

Figure 2.1   Incentives in a cost reimbursable contract for early completion

supervisory burden on the client in checking the contractor's actual costs, in identifying costs which should be disallowed and in negotiating variations to the target so it remains effective as an incentive. If all this is not done, then the contract will simply slide into straightforward cost reimbursement. On the other hand, to do it all in a timely and appropriate manner will add cost for the employer, who is unlikely to have the resources to do the work involved and will have to engage outside professional assistance probably in the form of quantity surveyors or cost engineers experienced in the type of work in question.

TERMS OF PAYMENT

Terms of payment are a matter on which the commercial, technical and financial sides of the employer's business may find themselves pulling in different directions. The employer may attain the best commercial and technical result if they offer the tenderers terms of payment which while providing the employer with reasonable contractual safeguards impose the minimum strain on the contractor's financial resources. There are a number of advantages to this approach:

1. The employer avoids having to restrict the tender list to large firms possessing the resources to finance the contract, whose overheads and prices are likely to be higher than those of smaller companies (this assumes, of course, that such smaller companies are otherwise technically and commercially competent to carry out the work).
2. It ensures that the tenderers do not have to inflate their tender prices by financing charges. In many instances, the rate of interest which the contractor has to pay when borrowing will be higher than that paid by the employer.
3. It gives encouragement to and allows the employer to take advantage of firms

possessing technical initiative who would otherwise be held back from expanding by lack of liquid cash.

4. The employer minimizes the risk of being saddled with a contractor who has insufficient cash with which to carry out the contract and of having therefore to either support the contractor financially or terminate the contract.

On the other hand, to offer such terms means that the purchaser has to finance the work in progress, tying up their own capital in advance of obtaining any return on the investment. It could therefore be argued that with a project such as a new factory or power plant it would impose the least financial strain on the employer if they could avoid paying anything at all until the project was earning money. There are also two other arguments which are often used to support the case for only paying at the end when the contract is complete:

1. Payment on completion provides the contractor with the best possible incentive to finish the whole of the work by the date for completion. It is far more effective than imposing liquidated damages for delay.

2. Paying monthly as the work proceeds, as is normal in building and civil engineering contracts, has encouraged the establishment of small contractors who do not possess the technical and managerial competence to undertake the work, tender low, uneconomic prices and lack the cash resources to fund the work when they run into difficulties. It is too easy to set up as a builder by hiring labour on a self-employed subcontract basis and the necessary plant, and buying materials on credit terms which mean that they are in fact paid for by the purchaser. Such firms do not last very long, but their presence while they are in business is one of the reasons why tender prices are uneconomic and too low to support the required level of investment, especially in training. They are also a prime cause of the adversarialism and claims culture prevalent in the industry.

There is some truth in both these arguments, but the practice in the construction industry is too well established. Even the Latham Report, *Constructing the Team* (1994), did not recommend the abolition of interim payments, although it did recommend that payments should be related to the completion of milestones or activities.

Merely financing the contractor by paying them monthly for the quantity of work performed, whether any item has been completed or not, is not considered to be to the purchaser's advantage.

Similarly, waiting to pay until completion of the whole of the works would lose purchasers the advantages identified at the beginning of this section and would be unlikely to be acceptable to the industry. In any event, under the Housing

Grants Construction and Regeneration Act 1998 if the contract is a construction contract as defined by the Act and will last more than 45 days, there must be provision for stage payments although an unscrupulous employer could find ways to defeat the intent of the Act. On balance and in conformity with the spirit of the Act and of the Latham Report the preferred solution is to pay against completion of defined activities as is provided for in Option A of the *Engineering and Construction Contract* (ICE 1995), 'Priced Contract with an Activity Schedule'. The contractor when tendering prepares the activity schedule although the purchaser when inviting tenders can state any particular activities which they wish to have priced or any activities which they wish to be grouped together. Each activity or a group of activities is then priced as a lump sum. On each assessment date, say monthly, the project manager determines which activities or group of activities have been completed and the contractor is paid for the completed work. It is important to note that payment is only made for completed activities or, where they are grouped, against completion of the group. There is no payment for a percentage complete. This method is suitable for building, mechanical and electrical engineering and process plant contracts.

However, as noted earlier, not all contracts can be tendered for on a lump sum basis. If it is impracticable to do so because of the uncertainties involved in assessing the quantities, so that a bill of approximate quantities is needed, then it is traditional to pay on a monthly basis the value of work which has been completed. However, the possibility should always be considered of tying in payment with the completion of certain milestones which can be identified from the programme. The milestone could be, for example, the construction of a foundation for a particular item of mechanical plant. Payment would then be made only against completion of that item ready to receive the plant.

Two problems particularly associated with monthly payment of remeasurement contracts are the practice of contractors to over-measure during early months of the contract and to front-end load by artificially increasing the rates for items of work carried out early. The use of an activity or milestone method of payment would overcome the first of these. The second can be avoided by allowing the contractor to identify as an activity, say, the preparation of the site.

DELAY IN PAYMENT

Where the contract provides for payment to be made against some clearly defined event, and for the payment to be within a specified period of that date, there is no excuse for delay in payment. The specified date may be either from the issue by the architect or engineer of a certificate of completion or from receipt by the purchaser of an invoice which the contractor was entitled to submit, depending on the contract. Late payment is quite simply a breach of contract, although one of the commonest committed. Many contracts do in fact provide for the payment of interest on delayed payments. Further, if payment is delayed after notice from the contractor for more than a specified period, the contractor may be entitled to suspend work or even to terminate the contract, although these rights do not exist at common law. If the contract does not provide a substantial contractual remedy for late payment, then the Late Payment of Commercial Debt (Interest) Act provides that interest shall be payable at 8 per cent above base rate in respect of late payments. The Act is now in force on contracts for the sale of goods or engineering and building works which are between a small business (less then 50 employees) and a large business (more than 50 employees) in respect of payments due from the large business. The Act does not specify a mandatory period for payment, although if no period is stated, then the period is 30 days from delivery or performance of the service. In practice a period of 30 days from the certificate of the event having been achieved should be sufficient for any well-organized employer. There is also now a limited right for the contractor to suspend performance of a construction contract under the Construction Industry Act if payment is delayed beyond final date for payment and no effective notice to withhold payment has been given.

ADVANCE PAYMENTS

The general rule is that payments made in advance of the contractor starting work or of delivery of equipment to site should be avoided so far as possible. If for commercial reasons such payments have to be made, then they should always be secured by a bond which is on first demand.

PROGRESS PAYMENTS DURING MANUFACTURE

On contracts which include the manufacture of plant, it is again suggested that progress payments in advance of the actual delivery of such plant to site should be avoided. The primary reason is the purchaser's lack of security for such payments and the difficulties of recovering them if the manufacturer gets into financial difficulties. If for commercial reasons it becomes necessary to make such payments, then:

- plant to at least the value of the payment should be identified, marked as such, separately stored and the contract should state that on payment it becomes the property of the purchaser;
- such plant should, however, also be stated in the contract to remain at the risk of the manufacturer until at the earliest it has been delivered to site and may

be depending upon the contract until the works as a whole have been accepted by the purchaser.

RETENTION MONEY

With contracts for building and civil engineering works and large contracts for supply and installation of plant and equipment, it is usual for the purchaser to retain a proportion of the contract price until the work has been completed, passed its tests (if any) and accepted by the purchaser. This percentage varies but is usually between 10 per cent and 20 per cent. On acceptance, half of this money is normally released and the balance held during the defects liability period as security for the performance by the contractor under their obligations to make good any latent defects which appear in the work. It is released at the end of this period provided that all defects have been remedied to the purchaser's satisfaction. Contractors often ask for the second half of the retention money to be released to them on completion against a bank guarantee. There can be no real objection to this, provided again that the bond is payable on first demand.

REFERENCES AND FURTHER READING

Institution of Civil Engineers (1995), *The Engineering and Construction Contract*, 2nd edition, Thomas Telford, London.

Institution of Civil Engineers (1999), *Conditions of Contract, Measurement Version*, 7th edition, Thomas Telford, London.

JCT80 (1980), *Joint Construction Tribunal Standard Forms of Contract*, 2nd edition, Royal Institute of British Architects, London.

Latham, Sir Michael (1994), *Constructing the Team: Final Report of the Government/Industry Review of Procurement and Contractual Arrangements in the UK Construction Industry*, The Stationery Office, London.

3 Farsighted project contract management

Rodney Turner

In the previous two chapters various contract structures and terms of payment were identified. There are three basic project contract structures:

- traditional structures;
- integrated structures;
- management structures;

and three basic forms of payment:

- cost plus;
- remeasurement;
- fixed price.

The different circumstances in which these contract structures and forms of payment are used were described in Chapter 2, where Peter Marsh suggested some criteria for selecting the appropriate form for a given situation. This chapter describes the results of recent research into contract selection and suggests a methodology. The aim is twofold:

1. To develop a cooperative project organization.
2. To appropriately allocate the management of risk.

It is a sad reality that the more common approach to contract management is to develop a project organization based on conflict. The owner and contractor try to outdo each other, to win a greater share of what they see as a fixed-sized cake in a win–lose battle. I think there is no such thing as a win–lose outcome, it is either win–win or lose–lose. The aim should be to develop a cooperative organization in which the owner and contractor work together to manage the risk and achieve a better result for both of them.

Projects are temporary organizations to which the owner assigns resources to achieve their development objectives. As with all organizations, it is in the owner's interest that all their 'employees' are motivated to achieve their objectives. It is through the project contracts that the owner employs outside resources to work on the project, and attempts to align the resources' objectives with their own by properly motivating them. This chapter will describe a schema for contracts which judges their ability to align the contractor's objectives with the owner's to create a cooperative project organization.

This *ex-ante* incentivization would be all that is necessary if the project conditions were entirely predictable throughout its life. However, projects are not that predictable. Thus farsighted contracts are necessary; contracts that are able to deal with any new risks or uncertainty that may arise as the project progresses, that are able to deal with unforeseen events, both adverse and beneficial. These farsighted contracts will be unavoidably incomplete; they will not be able to deal with every eventuality. *Ex-post* governance is needed to provide farsightedness and allow adaptation required to deal with incompleteness. A second schema will describe the nature of governance provided by different contract types and their ability to cover farsightedness and deal with incompleteness.

There are two views on risk. The first is that you should use fixed-price contracts on projects with low risk, remeasurement with intermediate risk and cost plus with high risk. However, this is not modern practice. The second is that you should assign risk where it is most appropriately controlled. The problem is that projects are non-linear, coupled systems. Reducing risk in one area can create an even greater risk in another. Risk needs to be managed as a whole, not piecemeal. This chapter will describe modern practice on choosing contract structures and payment terms to allocate risk on projects.

The next section recalls that a contract is the method by which the owner creates the project organization and that the aim should be to develop a cooperative organization, not a conflict one. It then describes the two schemas for providing *ex-ante* incentivization and *ex-post* governance on projects, and shows how these apply to the different contract structures and forms of payment described in the previous two chapters. It describes modern practice in choosing contract type to allocate risk, and then proposes a methodology to choose a contract strategy based on:

- who controls the risk: the client or contractor, or both;
- the complexity of the project;
- where the risk lies: in the project's product or process, or both.

PROJECT ORGANIZATION: COOPERATION OR CONFLICT?

There are two ways of viewing a project organization: the correct way and the normal way, respectively:

- a temporary organization through which the owner assembles resources and motivates them, in a climate of cooperation, to achieve their (the owner's) objectives;
- a marketplace, in which the owner attempts to buy the project's outputs at the cheapest possible price, in a climate of conflict with the contractors, in which one party is going to win and one lose.

In the more common approach, the client adopts the mindset that they are going to buy the project's outputs in the local bazaar, and they must negotiate hard to achieve the lowest possible price from the vendor (contractor). The negotiation is viewed as a win–lose game, in which one will gain the greatest share of a fixed cake. Therefore a climate of conflict develops where the client and contractor try to outdo each other which then spills over into project delivery, where the climate of mistrust continues. The client mistrusts the contractor throughout, assuming that the contractor is trying to claw back money through the project's delivery. This usually leads to a lose–lose outcome.

The project is a temporary organization, through which the client tries to assemble resources to achieve their development objectives. As in any organization, the owner should view the resources working for them as their employees (albeit this will be a temporary employment relationship), and motivate these employees to achieve their objectives. Because it is a temporary employment relationship, the owner will often employ resources from an agency, and will ask the agency (contractor) to do the work on their behalf. Effectively their 'employees' will be a company (contractor) rather than a person, what the Dutch would call a legal person rather than a natural person. But the owner should view these legal persons as much their employees as natural persons, and motivate them to achieve their project objectives.

Levitt and March (in Williamson 1995) say this about the purpose of organizing:

> The problem of organizing [is] seen as one of transforming a conflict (political) system into a cooperative (rational) one. A conflict system is one in which individuals have objectives that are not jointly consistent. It organizes through exchanges and other interactions between strategic actors. A cooperative system is one in which individuals act rationally in the name of a common objective.

The aim of project organization should be to create a cooperative system in which individuals, legal persons and natural persons work together in a rational way to achieve a common (the owner's) objective. It is through the project contracts that the owner creates the project organization and 'employs' legal persons (the contractors) to work on their projects. Therefore it is through the contracts that the owner should try to motivate the contractors to achieve their objectives, which is best done through a win–win game. Thus when developing a project contract strategy the owner should choose a contract type that develops an appropriate social relationship between themselves and the contractor, and provides incentives to motivate the contractor to achieve their objectives. Because projects are temporary organizations they entail risk and uncertainty (and sometimes opportunity). Thus to provide an appropriate incentive the contract needs to recognize this risk and include appropriate safeguards to protect the contractor (and indeed to enable the owner to share in the exploitation of any opportunities). The contract should be designed to encourage the owner and contractor to act rationally together to achieve their common objectives and the best outcome for both, within the context of the expected risk.

However, that rationality is almost certain to be bounded by human frailty (Williamson 1996). It is bounded by the project participants' inability to precisely and unambiguously:

- communicate with each other;
- process information to interpret events;
- foretell the future.

Therefore, not only does the contract strategy need to provide incentives and safeguards to deal with the risks as envisaged in advance (*ex-ante* incentivization), it must be flexible enough to deal with unforeseen circumstances as they arise; the *ex-ante* contract is unavoidably incomplete. In order to maintain a climate of mutual cooperation, the contract needs to be adapted to these circumstances through mutual agreement and cooperation, not through one party using them to make gains over the other party. The contract needs to provide a flexible, farsighted *ex-post* governance structure that:

1. Allows adaptations through mutual agreement.
2. Provides a communication structure to identify how the project is progressing, and to identify any problems that may arise so that they can be dealt with in a cooperative fashion.
3. Continues to provide an incentive for the contractor to deliver the client's objectives.
4. Does this without either party feeling the need to resort to the law (which automatically is a lose–lose scenario – the 'winning' party just losing less than the other).

36

A THEORY OF CONTRACTS: INCENTIVIZATION AND GOVERNANCE

Oliver Williamson (1995, 1996) suggests two schemas or vectors to describe the ability of contracts to provide *ex-ante* incentivization and flexible farsighted *ex-post* governance.

EX-ANTE INCENTIVIZATION

In the first schema, to provide *ex-ante* incentivization (Figure 3.1) the contract is described by three parameters:

- the reward it provides the contractor to share the owner's objectives and perform;
- the associated risk;
- the safeguard provided by the owner through the contract to shield the contractor from the risk.

Where there is no risk present, there is no need for any safeguard and the reward can be low. If there is risk present, there may or may not be a safeguard. If there is no safeguard, the contractor buys all the risk off the owner and a high reward is required. Where there is a safeguard, the owner underwrites the contractor's risk and the incentive can be lower. Note that in some cases the safeguard only

Risk	Present	High incentive	Medium incentive
	Absent	Low incentive	No safeguard or incentive necessary
		Absent	Present
		Safeguard	

Figure 3.1   A simple contractual schema for *ex-ante* incentivization

37

provides protection against extreme risk. For lower levels of uncertainty the contractor takes the risk. However, for extreme events, the client underwrites the contractor. This is the case with target price contracts, or where the contractor only claims for variations over a certain size. In these cases, the reward may be less than where there is no safeguard at all.

Williamson is writing about contracts for supply of a large number of units, not for one-off, unique, novel and transient projects. He assumes the cost of works is independent of the contract type, the natural costs associated with the task. The incentive is part of the transaction costs associated with the contract, that is additional costs over and above the basic cost of works (Cox and Thompson 1998). However, we shall see later that on some projects different contract structures and forms of payments can lead to different out-turn costs and the incentive can come from the contractor sharing in savings in the cost of works (even keeping all the savings on fixed-price contracts).

FLEXIBLE, FARSIGHTED, *EX-POST* GOVERNANCE

Although the schema above assumes a safeguard risk, it can really only deal with risks that are foreseen. If properly motivated, the project's participants should behave rationally towards a common (the owner's) objective. However, as Williamson suggests, because of human frailty their rationality is bounded mainly by their ability to communicate, to process information and to foresee the future. Thus every project contract is almost certainly incomplete. Farsighted, *ex-post* governance is required to deal with unforeseen circumstances. Williamson propounds four parameters to describe the ability of a contract form to provide flexible, farsighted, *ex-post* governance:

- the incentive intensity;
- the ease of making uncontested, bilateral adaptations to the contract;
- the reliance on monitoring and related administrative controls (transaction costs);
- the reliance on court ordering.

Incentive intensity   Greater incentive intensity will elicit greater performance and sustained effort from the contractor to achieve the owner's objectives, and greater flexibility in accepting changes to adapt to unforeseen circumstances.

Bi-lateral adaptation   This describes the ability of the parties to a contract mutually to accept changes. Some contracts inhibit changes, even if both parties are willing to accept them but others encourage them. Although this is described as 'bilateral adaptiveness', it is not always the case that both parties need to be party to the decision to adapt. It depends on the ability of parties to solve problems. We will see it is often the case that the client can make no contribution to problem solving. What is best for cooperation is to let the contractor get on with it and decide (within the constraints set by the incentive) on the preferred way of dealing with the changes.

Reliance on monitoring and administrative controls Some contract forms require very intrusive systems for monitoring and control, leading to high transaction costs, while others allow quite light control. On projects, these transaction costs associated with monitoring and control can be small when compared to the savings to the costs of works through appropriate motivation of the contractor. Thus incentive intensity has a stronger impact on project costs than reducing control procedures. However, if appropriate incentives are chosen, there may be no need for monitoring and control procedures since the contractor can be allowed to work unilaterally.

Reliance on court ordering If the contract discourages cooperation and encourages conflict, then it may be necessary for the client and contractor to settle their differences in court. Reliance on court ordering is a measure of how much the contract encourages client and contractor to cooperate and settle their differences of opinion in ways other than resorting to the law. If it is necessary to resort to the law, then the project has become a conflict system and all parties stand to lose, just some more or less than others.

CONTRACT TYPES AND A THEORY OF CONTRACTS

Traditional contract forms will now be compared to the two schemas above. By considering mainly forms of payment, a slightly wider view is given than that in Chapter 2. We will see that different contract structures attach naturally to forms of payment as we select contract types. The forms of payment considered are:

1. Cost-plus contracts
   - cost plus percentage fee (c+%f)
   - cost plus fixed fee (c+ff)
   - cost plus incentive fee (c+if)
   - alliance contracts, or cost plus gain share (alliance).
2. Remeasurement contracts
   - remeasurement based on a schedule of rates (r-sor), effectively cost plus

- remeasurement based on a bill of quantities (r-boq)
- remeasurement based on a bill of materials (r-bom), effectively fixed price plus variations.

3. Fixed-price contracts
    - fixed-price based on a detailed design (fpdd), effectively remeasurement
    - fixed-price design and build based on a scope design
    - fixed-price design and build based on cardinal points (a functional specification).

4. Others
    - target cost
    - time and materials to budget, or guaranteed maximum price.

The incentive profiles of the contract types are summarized in Figure 3.2 and the governance profiles in Figure 3.3. These tables also show the profiles of the traditional contract forms, markets and hierarchies described by Williamson (1995, 1996) for routine supply.

Contract form	Reward	Risk	Safeguard
Cost plus			
c+%f	High but misaligned	High	High
c+ff	Medium but misaligned	High	High
c+if	Medium	High	High
Alliance	Medium	High	Medium
Remeasurement			
r-sor	Low and misaligned	Low	High
r-boq	Low	Medium	Medium
r-bom	Low	Medium	Low
Fixed price			
build only	Low	Low	Low
specification a	Low	Low	Low
specification b	Medium	Medium	Low
cardinal points	High	High	Low (insurance)
Other			
target price	Medium	Medium	Medium
time and materials budget or gmp	Low	High	Low
Routine contracts			
market	High	Low	Low
hierarchy	Low	High	High

Figure 3.2   Contract forms and *ex-ante* incentivization

Contract form	Incentive intensity	Adaptiveness	Transaction costs	Court ordering
Cost plus				
c+%f	Misaligned	High	High	Low
c+ff	Low	High	High	Low
c+if	Medium	High	High	Low
Alliance	High	High	High	Low
Remeasurement				
r-sor	Misaligned	Medium	High	Low
r-boq	Low	Medium	Medium	Low
r-bom	Low	Medium	Low	Low
Fixed price				
build only	Low	Low	High	High
specification a	Low	Low	High	High
specification b	Medium	Medium	Medium	Medium
cardinal points	High	High	Low	Low
Other				
target price	Medium	Low	High	Medium
time and materials	Low	Low	High	High
to budget or gmp				
Routine contracts				
market	High	Low	Low	High
hierarchy	Low	High	High	Low

Figure 3.3   Contract forms and flexible, farsighted, *ex-post* governance

COST PLUS

Cost-plus fee

Incentive   These are conventionally adopted on contracts of high risk, where the cost-plus nature provides a high safeguard for the contractor. It could be said that this contract form yields a high reward for the contractor, but it is the wrong reward. With cost-plus percentage fee the motivation is for the contractor to overspend and go late. The reward is misaligned with the client's objectives and success criteria. With cost-plus fixed fee there is a very small incentive for the contractor to finish to cost, because the higher the cost the lower their percentage profit. With cost-plus incentive fee there is a medium-level incentive to achieve whatever success criteria the incentive is linked to: cost (usually); time (penalties for late completion); quality and performance; safety.

Governance   These contracts are very adaptive but also have very high costs of monitoring and control. However, once the mechanisms of monitoring and control have been put in place they remain fixed, regardless of the amount of risk encountered and adaptations required. Because of their flexibility disputes should be low and so there should be little reliance on court ordering. Nevertheless, mistrust of the contractor by the client can be high.

The profile is wrong, there is high risk, but also high safeguard and incentive, and the incentive is not directed at achieving the client's success criteria, finishing to time, cost and functionality. There is no motivation to reduce the cost and scope of work, the exact opposite in fact. It is appropriate to use this form of contract where:

● there is very high risk and uncertainty, and
● where the contractor can make no contribution to reducing either.

This form is used on construction management contracts where the client's design consultant does the design but the construction management contractor is responsible for procurement and construction site management. The construction manager then has no control over the scope. However:

● the construction manager is usually paid a fixed price (with incentives) for their role;
● the *Engineering and Construction Contract* (ICE 1995) recognizes that the construction manager needs to be given incentives to choose the cheapest subcontractor, not the easiest to manage;
● the construction manager also has no control over unit rates; for simple contracts or subcontracts where the contractor does have control over their unit rates and productivity, remeasurement contracts should be preferred to cost plus.

The other context where this type of contract has traditionally been used is in product development, specifically weapons system development. The thinking is that at the start of the product development process the scope of the project is unknown and so there is high risk. Therefore the safeguard of cost plus is built in, but the incentive is misaligned with the client's objectives. In recognition of the uncertain future the form is very flexible, but there are high transaction costs as a result.

Alliance

A variation of cost-plus contract is the alliance (Scott 2001). The client and contractor work together in a spirit of cooperation to reduce the scope of works and hence the price, and to achieve other key performance indicators set by the client, such as time, performance, safety and environmental standards. The client establishes a gain share fund which is split between the client and all the contractors working on the project according to their overall achievement against the client's performance indicators. This form of contract works only where both the client and the contractors can make a contribution to reducing risk and to achieving of the performance indicators.

Incentive   There is clearly much uncertainty in this type of project. It is only worth adopting where the client and contractor can achieve considerable potential cost savings, otherwise the high transaction costs cannot be justified. There are some safeguards built in:

- the client accepts some of the risk (and potential gains) through the sharing of the gain share fund;
- usually there is a cap on the downside risk borne by the contractor – above a certain level of loss they are borne entirely by the client.

Governance   There is high incentive intensity. The gain share fund, linked to the client's key performance criteria, provides high motivation to the contractor to achieve the client's objectives. There is also high flexibility, but with a price to pay in terms of high transaction costs. Recourse to the courts is avoided through an escalation procedure built into the alliance agreement.

Summary   In an alliance contract, properly implemented, the *ex-ante* incentivization and *ex-post* governance are well aligned. However, there are high transaction costs and these are necessary. This form of contract needs to be tightly managed. An alliance does not imply *laissez-faire* management.

REMEASUREMENT CONTRACTS

In remeasurement contracts the contractor is rewarded for the amount of work done, according to a pre-agreed formula.

Schedule of rates (SOR)   The amount of labour and materials used is measured and the contractor is paid according to agreed hourly and unit rates. This is effectively cost plus. There is no motivation on the contractor to control productivity levels. It suffers from all the problems of cost plus. There is a high safeguard, but the reward is not aligned to the client's performance criteria. There are high transaction costs, but the incentive is not aligned to the client's objectives. SOR should be used where the work and material requirements are very clearly defined, by the client or their design consultant, and contractors then provide agreed amounts of labour and material against industry standard rates.

Bill of quantities (BOQ)   Standard work elements are identified and the contractor is rewarded according to the number completed. The contractor is now motivated to control productivity levels. It is appropriate where a project consists of clearly identifiable work elements but the exact number is uncertain at the outset. Again, the client should not expect the contractor to suggest improvements for the benefit of the client, because that will actually reduce their profit. The contractor may try to find ways of improving the delivery of the work elements but will not pass those improvements on to the client. The contractor may even take shortcuts to the client's detriment. So there are medium-level transaction costs, again giving the client little benefit.

Bill of materials (BOM)   Standard larger work packages are identified and the contractor is rewarded according to the number completed. In this case, once the price for the work packages has been set the contractor is not motivated to suggest improvements. However, in the early stages of the project the client and contractor can work together to optimize the design of the work packages and the client can ask contractors to bid competitively for the work package rates. Transaction costs are now lower because there are much larger elements of work requiring less need for monitoring and control.

Remeasurement contracts are the closest in a project context to the market in routine supply, especially in the SOR and BOQ cases. In the former the client is buying labour and bulk materials in the bazaar, and in the latter they are buying standard components. Therefore these will be appropriate where there is low specificity and relatively high competition to provide the labour and materials or supply the standard project components. With the BOM form there will be higher specificity, requiring closer cooperation between client and contractor while the work packages are defined, but enabling lower monitoring and control costs once work starts.

FIXED-PRICE CONTRACTS

Fixed price based on a detail design

The client or their design consultant produces a detailed design of the project's output (facility) which is awarded to a construction contractor for delivery. The construction contract may either be bid under competitive tendering, or it may be awarded according to a standard schedule of rates or bill of quantities. Either way this is effectively a remeasurement contract, since any variations will be completed according to a schedule of rates or bill of quantities. However, variations will be sought by the contractor, since typically these contracts are bid under tight margins and so they will seek to increase their profit through variations. Variations will also equally be resisted by the client. These types of contract can lead to the greatest mistrust between client and contractor.

They are the worst form from the contractor's perspective. There is little reward and no safeguard, but little risk if the design is well done. Because of this, incentive intensity is low. There is little motivation for the contractor to achieve the client's objectives – they are just trying to do the minimum work for the minimum cost. There will be no adaptiveness unless the contractor sees it as a way of making extra money. Transaction costs are high, to process the variations that arise, and because there is a strong climate of mistrust there is a heavy reliance on the courts.

Design and build based on a scope design

The client, or a design consultant, performs an initial scoping design of the facility and the contractor is required to do the detail design and construction. If the scope of supply also includes commissioning, this type of contract is sometimes called *lump sum turnkey*. It is usually said that this type of contract is appropriate where it is possible to specify the final facility quite tightly and so the risk will be low. However, it can also be used where the facility can be specified quite tightly but there may be some uncertainty in the method of delivery, and only the contractor has the skills to reduce the risks. The client or their design consultant can make no contribution to the delivery of the plant.

If the risks are low, the safeguards will be low and the rewards low. Where risks are low, there will be several contractors able to do the work and so they will all bid with tight margins. The cooperative organization is best served by the client keeping well away from the project during its delivery so that the contractor is free to make whatever adaptations to the process of delivery they see fit. If margins are tight, the contractor may try to claw back additional profit through variations and that will increase transaction costs. However, if the client were to increase the contractor's profit to cover variations under a certain size, which are almost inevitable, transaction costs can be reduced. Built-in incentives to control variations can lead to a cheaper outcome.

Cardinal points or functional specification

The client specifies the functionality and key performance indicators (cardinal points) of the facility to be delivered by the project, but leaves it to the contractor to find the best solution both in terms of the design of the facility to achieve those, and the method of its delivery. This form is best used where there is uncertainty about how best to deliver the facility, and the client can make no contribution to solving that problem. The contractor buys all the risk through a fixed-price contract, and makes their reward by finding the best solution. This contract form was used in the case of the Botlek Tunnel under the Oude Maas River, part of the Betuweroute (Dutch High Speed Freight Line) from the port of Rotterdam to the German border. It gave the client a price lower than they could get by any other contract form, but still let the contractors make a reasonable reward through the solution they found to the project. They were motivated to reduce the scope of works by the form of contract.

Incentive   The contractor's risk is high, but there are suitable rewards. In the case of the project just described, by and large there were no safeguards. The contractors bought all the foreseeable risks but the client, the Dutch state-owned railways, underwrote some further low probability but high severity insurable risks. This enabled the contractors to bid a lower price than if they had underwritten those risks themselves. In the event, the risks were not encountered.

Governance   The contractor's incentive comes from their ability to find an effective solution to the problems, and so can be high. The form of contract is very adaptive because the contractor is left to work to find the best solution which means that transaction costs are low. If well formulated, there should be little need for recourse to the courts because the cardinal points can be quite clear. And if the extreme risks are properly underwritten, there should be no need to make claims.

OTHER FORMS OF CONTRACT

Target cost

A target price contract provides a fixed price for an agreed range of out-turn costs around the target price, where the client and contractor share the result of any underspend or overspend. Often the client also puts a cap on the contractor's exposure for overspend above an agreed level. Within the range this contract acts like a fixed-price contract. There is a potential for the contractor to achieve higher rewards, but at greater risk. The incentive intensity is higher than for fixed-price contracts and higher transactions costs are needed to monitor regular performance. However, with those monitoring and administrative procedures in place, variations are easier to process. These contracts can still lead to arguments requiring recourse to the courts, but because contractors are motivated to save cost, they will not be pursuing variations to increase their profits.

This contract form can lead to strong collaboration between client and contractor, as in the case of the alliance contract, since it is in both their interests to save cost. The *Engineering and Construction Contract* (ICE 1995) treats fixed price as a special case of target cost, with the target range extended to infinity. However, the two types of contract do have subtly different profiles and require different monitoring and control regimes.

Time and materials to budget or guaranteed maximum price

This contract form is a fool's game:

- contractors who accept it are fools because it is weighted heavily in favour of the client;
- clients who push it on their contractors are fools because contractors operating under it are completely demotivated and do not have the client's interests at heart.

The contract is cost plus to a target price and then fixed price beyond. The contractor takes on all the downside risk, but shares none of the upside opportunity.

Incentive   The contractor has no incentive to achieve the client's objectives. The rewards are low, the risks are high and there is no safeguard.

Governance   The governance structure has all the disadvantages of cost plus and fixed price with none of the advantages. The incentive intensity is low: the contractor makes big losses if the project is overspent, but small profits if it is underspent; and the more underspent the contract, the smaller the contractor's profits. High transaction costs are required to monitor what the contractor is actually spending, so the client can claw back money if they underspend. There is no adaptiveness. The contractor is totally unwilling to take on additional work and the client, to adopt this type of contract, must be in an uncompromising position. The reliance on court ordering will be high, as the contractor tries to prove that any overspend is due to the client's errors.

This contract form is conflict organization. It is lose–lose project management.

CHOOSING CONTRACT TYPES

How do you choose the appropriate type of contract for a particular project? Conventional wisdom is that contract type is dependent on the level of risk:

- At low levels of risk, fixed price is appropriate. The contractor takes little or no risk in buying the project and its associated risk off the client.
- At intermediate levels of risk, remeasurement is appropriate.
- At high levels of risk, cost plus is appropriate. It would be inappropriate to expect the contractor to bear risk which rightfully belongs to the client.

However, Turner and Simister (2001) showed that this does not fit current practice. By investigating a range of large construction and infrastructure projects from several European countries they showed that contract type tends to be chosen as follows:

1. Remeasurement contracts are used on low risk projects, but specifically where the contractor can make no contribution to the improvement of the design through construction knowledge. The client and their consultant complete the design without involving the contractor, and then appoint the contractor to complete the construction works, paying them according to industry standard schedules of rates or bills of quantities. This is the assumption behind the traditional procurement route (see Chapter 1) and the Institution of Civil Engineers standard form of contract (ICE 1995). They tend to be construction only contracts.
2. Fixed-price contracts are used where the client can make no contribution to the delivery of the project and the management of risk. The contractor buys the risk off the client and is then motivated to find the best way of completing the project independent of the client. The contractor can make good profits by finding the best solution, but the client often gets the project more cheaply than they would with other contract forms. They tend to be design and build or turnkey contracts.
3. Cost-plus contracts are used where both the client and contractor can work together to reduce the risk, but specifically the type is the alliance contract. The client and contractor (or contractors – there may be several) together find the best solution of the project. A gain share pot is created so that the client and all the contractors can share in the achievement of the client's objectives (reduced risk, reduced out-turn cost, and the achievement of other performance indicators).

Thus the form of contract is chosen to achieve goal alignment, dependent on who controls the risk: the client, the contractor or both together. Control over the risk tends to be linked to where the risk lies:

- If the risk lies in the method of delivering the project, then the contractor has best control over it and fixed-price contracts are best. If the product can be clearly specified (especially in the case of cardinal points procurement), and the uncertainty lies in how that product is best achieved, the contractor has control over the risk.

- If the risk lies in the product to be delivered (which means there will also be uncertainty in the work methods), then the client and the contractor both control the risk, and alliance contracts are best. Client and contractor now need to work together to reduce the risk.
- If the risk is low, the client and their consultant can develop the design package independently of the contractors and assign a prescribed package of work.

GOAL ALIGNMENT AND OPPORTUNISM

Thus the most significant issues when choosing a form of contract are achieving goal alignment between the client and the contractor and reducing the chance and benefit for opportunism by the contractor. The purpose of project organization and contract management is to create a cooperative system by achieving common objectives and by properly incentivizing the contractors. Goal alignment comes from aligning the three Ps for the project: process, product and purpose. The owner's profit comes from operating the product to achieve the purpose. The contractor's profit comes from undertaking the process to deliver the product. Goal alignment ensures that the right process is used to deliver the right product to achieve the client's desired purpose. Lack of goal alignment will result in maladaptation of one of the three Ps:

- *Maladaptation of the process:* the process does not deliver the product as designed.
- *Maladaptation of the product:* the product as designed does not meet the client's needs.
- *Maladaptation of the purpose:* the client's needs change from what was originally envisaged.

If the purpose, product and process are all well defined and unlikely to change, then a remeasurement contract is the best approach. The client (or their consultant) do the detail design, and the contractor is awarded the work, at a price defined by an agreed schedule of rates or bill of quantities and which gives the contractor a reasonable profit. However, this approach is unlikely to lead to any improvement in the project's design or cost. The contractor is not going to suggest any improvements unless they can share in the benefits. This is not just a lack of cooperation on behalf of the contractor. Remember that the first priority of the contractor's directors is to their shareholders. They are required to maximize profits for the shareholders. It would be a dereliction of duty to their shareholders to accept a remeasurement contract that did not allow them to share in cost reductions and then to suggest cost reductions. Client organizations need to recognize that. In the public sector, the government, out of a misguided sense of having to obtain the best value for taxpayers, often applies remeasurement contracts precisely, insisting that any cost reductions are clawed back from the contractors. This actually leads to the contracts being more expensive than they would be if the contractors were allowed to share in the improvements. Creating one-sided contracts leads to a conflict system, and increasing project costs. The contract does not have to be fair, just clear; but if it is clearly unfair, and the contractor is not left with the ability to manage risks to increase profits, then they will not share a common objective with the client. Further, late changes are likely to lead to inflated costs, not justified by any accruing benefits.

If the product and purpose are fairly predictable, particularly if the product can be defined by cardinal points, then a fixed-price contract can be the best way of ensuring the correct process is adopted. The contractor is made responsible for designing the best solution for delivering the project's product, and gains from any innovative solutions found. The client must not needlessly interfere in the contractor's work. Turner and Simister (2001) report one project manager who said:

> The client cannot be a control freak without taking a stick, and setting rules and regulations, and that will undermine the contractor's responsibility. The client will then be to blame for everything.

The client should be there to help the contractors if they get into difficulty, but leave them alone if that is what they want. Interference can lead to friction.

If the project's product is uncertain, or if the purpose changes because of market conditions, then a cost-plus contract based on an alliance may be best.

Finally, the client needs to put in place information systems to pick up opportunism by the contractor at an early stage, without interfering too much or acting as a control freak. With fixed price that is not necessary and administrative costs will be lower, as suggested in the previous section. It is necessary on remeasurement or cost-plus contracts, adding to the cost of their administration. However, on fixed-price contracts where there is potential maladaptation of the product or purpose, a configuration management process will be necessary to refine the product. That process will increase the administration costs and the potential cost of variations, leading to the undermining of the cost advantage of the fixed-price contract if the uncertainty of the product unexpectedly turns out to be high.

A STRATEGY FOR PROJECT CONTRACT SELECTION

We can now develop a methodology for project contract selection based on the need to:

- provide the contractor with incentive to achieve the client's objectives;
- provide flexible, farsighted governance to deal with incompleteness, but at minimum transaction costs.

The methodology (see Figure 3.4) depends on several questions:

1. Who controls the risk?
   - the client
   - the contractor
   - both.

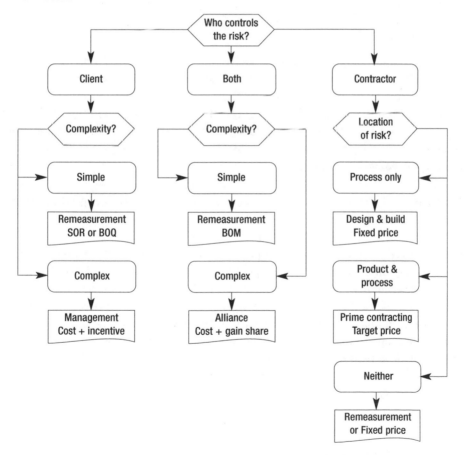

Figure 3.4 Methodology for project contract selection

2. The nature of the project?
   ● simple
   ● large, complex, multi-stage.
3. The location of the uncertainty?
   ● in the project's product
   ● in the process of delivering the product
   ● both
   ● neither.

CLIENT CONTROLS THE RISK

If the client (or their consultant) controls the risk, then the appropriate types of contract are cost-plus incentive fee or remeasurement depending on the complexity.

Low complexity

For low complexity projects a remeasurement contract based on a schedule of rates or bill of quantities is appropriate. The Dutch rail infrastructure company operates a take-it-or-leave-it approach. The client's consultant designs the facility, which is priced using a standard schedule of rates or bill of quantities. That gives a price for the job, which the contractor accepts or refuses. Any variations are priced using the standard schedule. This is effectively fixed price with flexibility built in to deal with variations.

Incentive　The risk is low, there is a small safeguard in the accepted variations, the rewards are low.

Governance　There is an incentive to control cost, and rewards/penalties for time, quality and safety can be built in if needed. There is some flexibility in the accepted variations. The administrative procedures to monitor variations can be routine, but if the specification is critical, costly inspection procedures will be necessary. Penalties built into reward structure for poor performance post commissioning are too late and may not compensate for poor performance. There should be little recourse to the courts if the variation process works.

High complexity

For high complexity projects a cost-plus incentive fee management contract, (see Chapter 1) may be appropriate. The contractor is paid a fixed price with incentive for their contribution, which is the procurement of subcontractors and the management of the work. The client pays the cost of the subcontractors, either directly or via the main contractor. Any construction work done by the main contractor will probably be paid for on a remeasurement basis, as above.

Incentive   The risk is high, but there is a safeguard in the form of the cost-plus contract. The rewards should be medium.

Governance   With an incentive fee, there is an incentive to control cost, and rewards/penalties for time, quality and safety can be built in if needed. There is total flexibility in the cost of subcontracts. The administrative procedures to monitor the contract are part of the project monitoring, the responsibility of the management contractor. The main contractor has no incentive to cut corners but the subcontractors might, so if the specification is critical, costly inspection procedures will be necessary. There should be little need for recourse to the courts if the process works.

There have been certain cases where the client has deliberately underestimated the scope of the work and the management contractors find themselves managing a job three times as large as they expected for a fixed fee. That is immoral and any client who has done that will probably not flexibly adjust the fee. If it truly was a mistake, then flexibility may need to be built into the contract so that the fee can be reviewed if it does not reflect the scope of work as it turned out. This would be the case if there was very high uncertainty in the extent of the project, and the result would be a cost-plus percentage fee contract. But changes and adjustments to the fee must be strictly monitored.

CONTRACTOR CONTROLS THE RISK

Here the type of contract depends on where the risk is:

- in the process;
- in the product and process (product only implies product and process);
- neither.

Risk in the process

The project's product can be clearly defined; the uncertainty lies in how it is to be delivered. The contractor has control over that risk. The most appropriate contract is fixed-price design and build, with the product defined by cardinal points. (This type of contract is called design and build in the building industry.

In the engineering construction industry it is called turnkey or engineering, procurement and construction (EPC) (see Chapter 1).

Incentive   The contractor's reward derives from finding the optimum solution to the delivery of the project. Substantial reward can derive from finding a good, cost-effective solution.

Governance   The incentive to find a good solution is high. Sometimes this is the only way the client can afford the project. Flexibility is high if the client leaves the contractor alone. If the client meddles, it can become expensive. Monitoring and control costs are required to monitor the project anyway, so transaction costs are low. Acceptance tests will check that the functional specification has been delivered. Again, post-completion penalties for poor performance will not compensate the client. If the functional specification is well defined, there should be little need for recourse to the courts.

Risk in the product and the process

If there is risk in the product that the client cannot control, then the client has a functional requirement but no skill in house to deliver it. If there is uncertainty in the product, then there must also be uncertainty in the process. A common approach in this case is prime contracting with a target price contract. It is expected that the cost of the project can be predicted within certain ranges, and within that range the contract is fixed price. Outside that range the client and contractor share any savings if the project turns out easier than expected or any overspend if it turns out more expensive. There is usually a cap on the contractor's exposure, above which the contract becomes remeasurement and the risk reverts to the client.

Incentive   If the project hits the target cost, the contractor can make useful profits. There is an opportunity to make greater profits with a downside risk for less profit or even loss. The cap provides a safeguard.

Governance   The incentive to perform is high. Flexibility is best served by the client remaining aloof, but being on call if required. Costs must be monitored, however, so transaction costs are high. With a good relationship, there should be no need for recourse to the courts.

Design only contracts by the client's consultant also fall into this category. It is normal for these contracts to be done on time and materials (remeasurement based on a schedule of rates). Careful monitoring will ensure that the work done is essential. The client is very dependent on the consultant. The consultant's professional reputation motivates them to work in the client's best interest. The contractor's profit margin will either be built into the schedule of rates, or be an added percentage, so this arrangement is very close to cost-plus percentage fee except that the unit rates are set in advance. There may be no other option for a design only contract, but if the consultant becomes manager of the construction phase, a fixed fee, or fixed-price contract, or standard schedule of rates for the works should be adopted (see above).

Incentive   The rewards are useful, the risks can be high, but safeguards exist. The consultant's professional reputation is also part of the reward structure.

Governance   Unfortunately, the consultant is incentivized to expand the work, but their professional reputation motivates them to achieve the client's objectives. Flexibility is high, with a professional relationship between client and contractor enabling them to work in harmony. Monitoring and control costs need to be high, to check that only necessary work is done, and that it is done effectively and efficiently. The consultant's professional reputation reduces the need to take recourse to the courts.

Little risk

A fixed-price or remeasurement contract can be used, as described above under 'Risk in the process' or 'Low complexity', respectively.

SHARED RISK

If the risk is shared, then again the strategy depends on whether the complexity is high or low.

Low complexity

If the complexity is low, the contract form adopted could be remeasurement, fixed price or target price, depending on where the balance of the residual risk lies – with the client, with the contractor, in the process or the product. The considerations above apply.

High complexity

If the complexity is high, the appropriate form of contract is an alliance (Scott 2001 and Chapter 6).

Incentive   The rewards from an alliance contract can be high for both the client and contractor, if there is a successful outcome. The risks can be high but there is a safeguard in the form of:

- shared problem-solving;
- shared rewards;
- ensuring that the best result is achieved for the project as a whole and not any parties (client or contractors) individually.

Governance   The incentive is high and there is high flexibility, but there are high transaction costs. This usually means that alliance contracts can only be used on larger projects. (Scott suggests they should be greater than $US 15 million.) However that implies that the project is complex. With experience they can be applied to smaller projects.

CONCLUSIONS

This chapter adopts the premise that the purpose of project organization is to create a cooperative working relationship between all the parties involved, especially the owner and their contractors. The contracts are the method by which the owner creates the project organization and brings the contractors in. Therefore the contracts should aim to align the contractors' objectives with the owner's, by providing appropriate incentives.

A three-dimensional schema (reward, risk, safeguard) was used to analyse the efficacy of different contract types. Contractors will behave rationally to optimize their economic position, so the owner needs to ensure that all their contractors' economic positions are aligned with theirs.

Project contracts are also unavoidably incomplete. Bounded rationality means that people would like to behave rationally, but through human frailty will not do so perfectly. Bounded rationality is caused by an inability to communicate and process all information, and foresee the future. Thus the contracts should also be able to respond to unforeseen circumstance. A four-dimensional schema (incentive intensity, adaptiveness, reliance on monitoring and control, reliance on the courts) analyses the governance efficacy of the different contract types.

The results of this analysis suggest a methodology for contract selection, depending on whether the risk is controlled by the client or the contractor, whether the project is simple or complex, and whether the risk is on the project's product, method of delivery or both.

REFERENCES AND FURTHER READING

Cox, A. and Thompson, I. (1998), *Contracting for Business Success*, Thomas Telford, London.

Institution of Civil Engineers (1995), *The Engineering and Construction Contract*, 2nd edition, Thomas Telford, London.

Institution of Civil Engineers (1999), *Conditions of Contract: Measurement Version*, 7th edition, Thomas Telford, London.

Scott, R. (ed.) (2001), *Partnering in Europe: Incentive based Alliancing for Projects*, Thomas Telford, London.

Turner, J. R. and Müller, R. M. (2003), 'On the nature of projects as temporary organizations', *International Journal of Project Management*, 21(1), 1–8.

Turner, J. R. and Simister, S. J. (2001), 'Project contract management: a transaction cost perspective', *International Journal of Project Management*, 19(8), 457–64.

Williamson, O. E. (1995), *Organization Theory: from Chester Barnard to the Present and Beyond, expanded edition*, Oxford University Press, New York.

Williamson, O. E. (1996), *The Mechanisms of Governance*, Oxford University Press, New York.

4 Standard forms of contract

Stephen Simister and Rodney Turner

We saw in Chapter 1 that the relationship between the client and the supplier of goods and services is generally controlled by means of a contract. The contract sets out the intentions of the two parties, so should any dispute arise the true meaning of the roles and responsibilities of both sides is clear. At least that is the intention. However, even when intentions are written down their meaning is often unclear and expensive court cases are brought to try to resolve disputes. Generally the parties to a contract do not want to end up in court and they will seek to establish a contract that is acceptable to both sides and makes their intentions clear. This is the role of the standard form of contract.

This chapter compares bespoke and standard forms of contract and describes some of the standard forms available.

BESPOKE VS STANDARD FORMS OF CONTRACT

Bespoke contracts are written specifically to suit the circumstances of the relationship they are to control. For instance, if you wanted an extension built on your house, you might draw up a bespoke contract with a local builder which sets out various facets of the relationship such as:

- when the builder is to start and finish the project;
- how much the builder will get paid and when; and
- what happens if the extension is not to the agreed quality standard.

The bespoke contract is tailored to suit the exact circumstances for which it was written. On a small undertaking such as a house extension the time and effort required to write such a document should not be too arduous. However, it is a legal document and advice should be sought from an appropriate expert, and this will obviously add cost to the task. For a more complex undertaking the drafting of a bespoke contract can be extremely arduous as well as expensive.

The alternative to bespoke contracts are standard forms of contract. Standard forms are produced within a range of industries typically by professional bodies serving those industries or by committees specifically set up for the purpose. The building and construction industry seems to be the best served by standard forms with a huge number available. Where a standard form of contract is available that suits your project, it is generally considered best to use that instead of a bespoke contract. The rationale behind this is outlined below.

WHY USE STANDARD FORMS?

Standard forms of contract are generally prepared by an organization or body which has a genuine interest in a particular industry. To produce a standard form of contract requires considerable effort and is something that is not undertaken lightly. For instance, in 1998 the UK's Association for Project Management published standard terms for the appointment of a project manager (see Chapter 1). These standard terms took some two years to draft. They consist of two parts, the first part is the agreement and the second is an industry specific schedule of service; its arrangement is shown in Figure 4.1. By splitting the terms into two halves, the APM is able to cover all industries within which project managers may work. The terms were written in response to a request from industry. This brings the APM in line with just about all other professional bodies which produce their own standard terms of appointment, for example architects, engineers, lawyers, surveyors, etc.

As previously mentioned, the building and construction industry has produced a wide range of standard forms of contract. In the UK the most widely known are the suite produced by the Joint Contracts Tribunal (JCT). This body is drawn up from a range of representative professional and trade bodies within the construction industry. JCT produces more than sixty forms of contract and subcontract together with guidance notes on their use. Figure 4.2 shows standard forms for various branches of the construction industry and related industries in the UK.

Standard forms of contract purport to provide a representative viewpoint of the industry which they serve. Rather than favour one particular party to the contract, standard forms should represent both parties on an equal and fair basis by providing for an equitable distribution of risk. Of course, this nirvana does not suit everybody, and in the UK some clients produce their own standard forms. For instance, Defence Estates looks after all MOD property

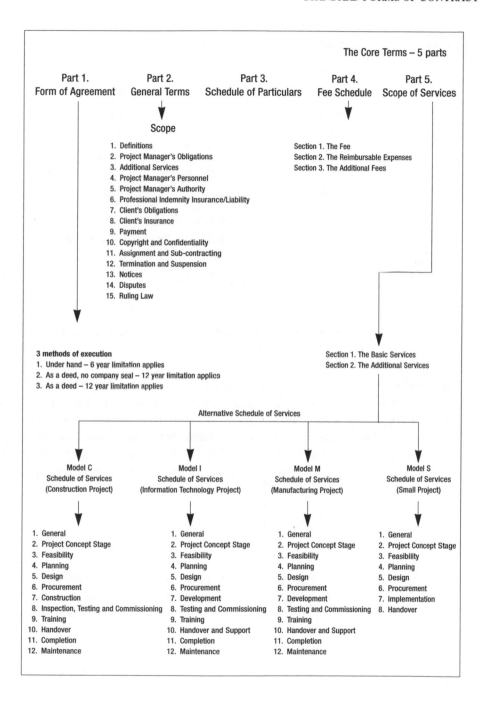

Figure 4.1   APM standard terms for the appointment of a project manager

Industry	Institutions	Standard form	Type
Project management	APM	Project management	Professional services
Building	JCT	JCT SF 98 (6 versions)	Price
	JCT	JCT CD 98	Price
	JCT	JCT IFC 98	Price
	JCT	JCT MC 98	Price
	JCT	JCT Prime Cost 98	Prime cost
	JCT	JCT Measured Term 98	Remeasurement
	RICS	Project Management	Professional services
Process	IChemE	Red Book	Price
		Green Book	Cost
		Yellow Book	Subcontract
Civil construction	ICE	ICE 7th	Remeasurement
		ICE D&C	Price
		NEC	Variable
Mechanical and Electrical	IMechE, IEE	MFI	Price

Figure 4.2 Standard forms of contract produced by the construction and engineering industries in the UK

and its form of contract called DEFCON 2000 favours the client to the extent that the contractor carries quite a high proportion of risk. The counter-argument is that contractors will not sign contracts they are not comfortable with. However, the balance of power lies fairly with the client and as the contract comes into use there will inevitably be acrimonious disputes which lead to court cases which perhaps a less adversarial approach may have prevented.

SUMMARY

Standard forms of contract are available in the majority of industries and their use is to be preferred over a bespoke form. By using standard forms, clients are demonstrating that they wish to abide by industry standards and not impose unfair terms that shift the balance of power too much in their favour.

REFERENCES AND FURTHER READING

Association for Project Management (1998), *Standard Terms for the Appointment of a Project Manager*, Association for Project Management, High Wycombe.

CIRIA 85 (1982), *Target and Cost Reimbursable Construction Contracts*, Construction Industry Research and Information Association, Report No. 85.

CIRIA 100 (1983), *Management Contracting*, Construction Industry Research and Information Association, Report No. 100.

Dingle, J., Topping, D. and Watkinson, M. (1995), 'Procurement and contract strategy', in J. R. Turner (ed.), *The Commercial Project Manager*, McGraw-Hill, London.

Institution of Chemical Engineers (1981), *Model Forms of Conditions of Contract for Process Plant, Lump Sum Contracts (Red Book)*, Institution of Chemical Engineers, Rugby.

Institution of Chemical Engineers (1992a), *Model Forms of Conditions of Contract for Process Plant, Reimbursable Contracts (Green Book)*, Institution of Chemical Engineers, Rugby.

Institution of Chemical Engineers (1992b), *Model Forms of Conditions of Contract for Process Plant, Subcontracts (Yellow Book)*, Institution of Chemical Engineers, Rugby.

Institution of Civil Engineers (1995), *The Engineering and Construction Contract*, 2nd edition, Thomas Telford, London.

Institution of Civil Engineers (1999), *Conditions of Contract: Measurement Version*, 7th edition, Thomas Telford, London.

Institution of Mechanical Engineers (1992), *MFI Model Forms of Contract*, MEP Ltd, Bury St Edmunds.

JCT 80 (1980), *Joint Construction Tribunal Standard Forms of Contract*, 2nd edition, Royal Institute of British Architects, London.

Royal Institute of Chartered Surveyors (1992), *Project Management Agreement and Conditions of Engagement*, 2nd edition, Royal Institute of Chartered Surveyors, London.

Wright, D. (1993), *Model Forms of Conditions of Contract for Process Plant, an Engineer's Guide*, Institution of Chemical Engineers, Rugby.

5 Contract law

Peter Marsh

This chapter provides a layman's guide to the main points of English contract law as it applies to commercial organizations. It in no way replaces the need for legal consultation in case of difficulty or dispute. If such cases do arise, then it is essential to seek professional legal advice at the earliest opportunity, before action is taken which may damage your company's position. This chapter considers the essential elements of a contract, factors which make a contract invalid and the terms or conditions and warranties.

CONTRACT FORMATION

There are four essential elements for a binding contract to be formed between two companies:

1. Offer.
2. Acceptance.
3. The intention to be legally bound.
4. Consideration.

OFFER

An offer in law is both a statement of the terms upon which a party is willing to contract and an expression of willingness to do so if an acceptance is given of those terms. It must be distinguished from an 'invitation to treat' (of which the classic example is the display of goods in a shop window), which is an indication of the terms upon which the seller is willing to do business, but not that they would accept any offer that was made. The commercial significance of this distinction is that a price list issued generally by a seller does not constitute an offer unless it is clearly evident from the terms of the price list that the seller intends to be bound by any order which the buyer places. An offer can be withdrawn at any time before it is accepted unless there is a separate contract under which the seller undertakes to keep it open for a certain period. This is because any promise made by the seller in a quotation to keep the offer open for, say, 60 days would not be binding, because it would not be supported by consideration (see below). However, withdrawal of the offer (revocation as it is often termed) is only effective when it has actually been received by the person to whom the offer was made. Accordingly, if an offer is accepted prior to the receipt of the notice of revocation, then a valid contract exists and the purported revocation is of no effect.

ACCEPTANCE

An acceptance of an offer becomes effective when it has been communicated to the person who made the offer. Assuming the offer has been sent by post, the acceptance has been communicated when the return letter is addressed, properly stamped and posted. Where the acceptance is by e-mail or facsimile, then the timing of acceptance is when the message is received on the machine of the person making the offer during normal working hours for that business. If the message is received outside these hours, it becomes effective at the moment the office reopens. The principal difficulty with acceptance is that to be effective in creating a contract its terms must coincide with those of the offer. Very often this is not the case. The seller makes an offer on their terms of sale and the buyer purports to accept but on their terms of purchase. In law such an 'acceptance' is classified as a counter-offer which the seller is free to accept or reject. At that stage, no contract exists and there are three possibilities:

1. Nothing is done to resolve the matter but in due course the goods are delivered and accepted by the buyer. By delivering the goods, the seller is regarded as having accepted the buyer's terms by conduct. This would not apply if the goods were accompanied by a delivery note referring to the seller's conditions which the buyer accepted.
2. The supplier returns a tear-off acceptance slip which was part of the buyer's order and which states that the supplier accepts the order on the buyer's conditions. The contract will then be on the buyer's conditions. This will be so even if the seller returns the slip with a letter which refers back to the seller's tender. This was interpreted by the court in *Butler Machine Tool Co. Ltd* v. *Ex-Cell-O Corporation* as only being a reference to the price and identity of the goods.

3. The seller can only protect themselves by referring in the letter specifically to their acceptance being on their terms of sale. This would then amount to a counter-offer which the buyer could either accept or reject. If the buyer did nothing and there was no further discussion of the terms of contract, then no contract would be formed until there was acceptance by conduct, for example by the buyer taking delivery of the goods.

INTENTION TO BE LEGALLY BOUND

Normally this requirement is easily satisfied where the transaction is between two commercial organizations. The parties may, however, not wish their agreement to be legally binding, and if they state so expressly, then the court will give effect to this. This is rare but it has happened with so-called 'Letters of Comfort' issued by banks when they have not been willing to give a guarantee of financial support.

More common are instances where one of the parties indicates that they have no intention to be legally bound by making their offer 'subject to contract'. There can then be no binding agreement until the parties have entered into a formal contract and, with sales of land, contracts have been exchanged.

Where the parties have left open important matters for future agreement, the court may also decide that the parties did not intend to be bound until such matters had been agreed. Similarly, an agreement to negotiate is not a contract because it is too uncertain to be enforced. To make the agreement binding, it would be necessary to establish in the contract a mechanism for settling the matters left to be agreed by reference to a third party whose decision the parties agree to accept as final and binding.

CONSIDERATION

Consideration is a highly technical concept peculiar to common law. It requires that for a binding contract to arise, an act or promise of one party must have been given in exchange for an act or promise by the other. Note, the consideration must exist; it does not need to be adequate. It cannot be claimed that a contract did not exist because the consideration was not adequate recompense for the offer. Normally there is no problem about consideration in a commercial contract, since the seller undertakes to supply the goods or do the work in consideration of the promise of payment by the purchaser. However, there are four situations in which the doctrine can have commercial significance.

Standing offers

Tenders are sometimes invited for an indefinite quantity of goods which the purchaser thinks they may require over a period of time. Unless the invitation states to the contrary, the purchaser by accepting such a tender does not bind themselves to order anything and is under no liability to the successful tenderer until they actually do place an order. Similarly, unless they have given consideration for keeping their offer open, the supplier may withdraw their tender at any time, but is obliged to fulfil any order which is placed before they do withdraw.

Promises to keep offers open

We saw above that a statement in a tender such as 'our offer is valid for 60 days' is not binding on the tenderer and they may withdraw it at any time before it is accepted. The reason is simply that the purchaser has given no consideration for the promise. It is possible for the purchaser to create consideration and in effect turn the offer into an option. Moreover, since the consideration need not be adequate, the amount could be largely nominal, say £5.

Promise post-contract to pay bonuses

The rule has been that when A is bound by a contract to perform certain obligations for B, then A's performance of their obligations could not provide consideration for a promise by B to make additional payments. However, it has now been established that if B's promise to pay is not due to pressure brought by A amounting to economic duress, and B gains practical benefits from the promise, then the promise is enforceable. The practical benefits obtained by B from A's performance on the original contract provide the consideration. This was established in a case in which a subcontractor who was in financial difficulties and likely to complete the work late was promised a bonus if they completed on time. By obtaining completion of the subcontract work to time, the main contractor obtained practical benefits, in particular they avoided having to pay damages for delay (*Williams* v. *Roffey Bros & Nicholls (Contractor) Ltd* (1991)).

Payment of lesser sum than a liquidated debt

If one party to a contract agrees to accept a lesser sum in settlement of a liquidated amount which is due to them, then that agreement will not be binding unless supported by some consideration other than the payment itself. Such consideration could be payment at an earlier date than required under the contract or the performance by the debtor of some other obligation of benefit to the creditor. In the absence of any consideration, the creditor can sue for the balance of the liquidated amount. In *D & C Builders* v. *Rees*, a firm of builders in severe financial difficulties accepted a payment of £300 in full settlement of the amount of £482 which they were owed. It was held by the Court of Appeal that they were entitled to recover the balance.

LETTERS OF INTENT

Like many other expressions in common commercial use, letters of intent have no distinct legal meaning. In order to determine what the parties meant when issuing and acting upon a letter of intent it is necessary to examine objectively what the parties did and said. The following are therefore only guidelines:

1. Generally a letter of intent does not give rise to any legal obligation on the part of either party. It is simply an expression of present intentions.
2. However, in addition to expressing an intention to award the contract to the supplier, the letter of intent may go on to authorize the supplier pending conclusion of negotiations to do certain work or purchase materials. If the supplier does so, but the contract is never concluded because the parties never reach agreement, then the purchaser is bound to pay a reasonable sum for the work done or materials supplied. However, since there never was a contract between them the supplier is under no contractual liabilities as regards defects in the work or as to the time of its completion.

INVALIDITY FACTORS AND FRUSTRATION

After its formation, a contract may be upset by one of several factors. These may be conveniently grouped together as:

- mistake;
- misrepresentation;
- duress;
- frustration.

MISTAKE

Only very rarely will a contract be held to be void or non-voidable for mistake. The mistake must be something fundamental, such as the existence of the goods, or where there is such confusion between the parties that there cannot objectively be said to be any agreement between them. A mistake as to quality will only ever upset the contract if it concerns some fundamental quality without which the goods would be essentially different from those which they were believed to be.

MISREPRESENTATION

Although there are four classes of misrepresentation – fraudulent, innocent, negligent and under the Misrepresentation Act 1967 – it is only the last which is of commercial significance in the law of contract. Negligent misrepresentation belongs to the law of tort with which we are not concerned. It is a misrepresentation under the Act if the statement is false and the party making it cannot show that he or she had reasonable grounds for believing it to be true. The other party's remedy is to recover damages.

DURESS

A contract is only valid if is entered into freely and voluntarily. Physical pressure to persuade someone to enter into a contract is fortunately very rare but there is now recognized a new category of duress, namely economic duress. This arises when the will of one party has been coerced by that of the other and the pressure exerted is illegitimate, such as a refusal by one party to carry out the contract unless a new contract is made under which they are paid more money. The effect of economic duress is to make the contract voidable and the innocent party can recover any payments made as a result of the duress. Mere commercial pressure will not be sufficient to constitute duress, nor will the fact that the one party has had to agree to harsh terms because of the weakness of their bargaining position.

FRUSTRATION

A contract will only be considered as frustrated, and therefore at an end, if it becomes impossible for it to be performed by reason of an event beyond the control of the parties. It is not sufficient that its performance for one party becomes more difficult or more expensive.

CONDITIONS AND WARRANTY

English law draws a distinction between two types of terms of contract, conditions and warranty. Conditions are essential terms, the breach of which allows the injured party both to rescind the contract and to claim damages. A warranty is a lesser term for the breach of which the only remedy is in damages. However, the meaning of the terms in any given contract is a matter of construction. The court may well decide that looked at objectively a term described as a 'condition' can only have been meant as a lesser term so its breach gives rise to no right to rescind the contract. Equally the use of the term 'warrant' in a contract may be held to be equivalent to guarantee and its breach give rise to a right to rescind. However, all the provisions of the Sale of Goods Act 1979 relating to quality and fitness for purpose are described by the Act as conditions. In insurance law, the opposite meaning is given to the term 'warranty', which is used to describe an essential term of the insurance policy. More recently the courts have introduced the concept of intermediate or innominate terms, the breach of which when it occurs may be either so serious that it would justify rescission or only serious enough to justify a remedy in damages alone.

THE CONTRACT PRICE

If a lump sum quotation is submitted and accepted, the contractor or supplier is obliged to complete the work or supply the goods without additional payment, even if doing so becomes more difficult or entails work beyond what they originally envisaged, unless the contract provides otherwise or there was misrepresentation on the part of the purchaser. In an old case involving a lump sum contract to build a house, flooring was omitted from the specification and it was held that the contractor must put it in without additional payment as it was clearly indispensably necessary to complete the house. Subject to the express terms of the contract, the entitlement of the contractor or supplier to payment of the contract price arises when they have performed the contract. However, there is a difference between contracts for work and materials such as building contracts and those for the supply of goods:

1. With a contract for work and materials, the contractor is normally entitled to payment when they have substantially completed the work, even if there are some minor defects or omissions for which the purchaser is entitled to make a reasonable deduction until the work is completed. Only if, as rarely happens today, the contract is construed as an entire contract, is the contractor not entitled to any payment until they have completed satisfactorily all the work which was required under the contract.
2. With a contract for the sale of goods, unless the contract expressly provides otherwise, the seller's obligations as to the quality of the goods and their compliance with the contract description are conditions of the contract. If that is breached, the purchaser is entitled to reject the goods (unless section 15A of the Sale of Goods Amendment Act 1994 applies). So normally there is

no obligation to make payment until goods complying wholly with the contract have been delivered, unless the purchaser is willing to accept them in their defective condition and offset or counterclaim for the reduction in value.

PASSING OF PROPERTY

The general rules for the passing of property are laid down under the Sale of Goods Act 1979. The Act draws a distinction between specific goods and those which are unascertained. Specific goods are those which are identified and agreed upon at the time of the contract. Unascertained goods are those which are either generic, say 100 tons of cement, or still to be manufactured or part of an undivided bulk. Section 17 of the Act sets out the rules which are to apply to the two categories of goods unless the contract states otherwise. With specific goods which are in a deliverable state the property passes when the contract is made regardless of whether delivery or payment is postponed. The property in unascertained goods passes when they have been unconditionally appropriated to the contract. This means that the goods must be irrevocably attached to the contract so that it is those goods and no others which are the subject of the sale and the seller has completed all their contractual obligations and so notified the purchaser.

The fact that the property in the goods has passed to the purchaser, but they have not yet paid for them, leaves the seller in a vulnerable position if the purchaser were to go bankrupt or into liquidation. For that reason, clauses which provide for the reservation of title until payment has been received in full are popular with sellers. The legal effect of any such clause depends on the way it is drafted and can raise complex problems. The following is therefore only a brief outline:

1. Where the goods unaltered are still in the buyer's possession, the seller will be entitled to recover them. If the clause so provides, this right will enable the seller to recover not only those particular goods, but all others which they have sold to the purchaser and for which payment has not been made; the so-called all sums clause. This is particularly important to the seller where they are making regular deliveries.
2. If the goods have been used in the manufacture of other products, so that they no longer have a separate identity, then the seller loses their right to recover them.
3. If, unusually, the clause provides that the purchaser holds the goods as bailee for the seller, and is under a fiduciary duty to account to the seller for the whole of the proceeds of sale, the seller may have the right to recover such

proceeds, if they have been placed in a separate bank account and so can be identified.

PASSING OF RISK

One reason for the importance of the clause relating to the passing of property is that, unless a contract provides otherwise, the risk in the goods passes to the purchaser at the same time as the property passes. Thus, if the seller introduces a clause into the contract under which the property in the goods does not pass until they have been paid, even once they have been delivered, then they should ensure that the risk in the goods passes to the purchaser on delivery. The purchaser is then responsible, say, to have them insured against theft or damage. Likewise, a buyer who is going to make payments while the goods are still in the course of manufacture should provide for the property in the goods to pass to them on payment, but that the risk should remain with the seller until after delivery.

DELIVERY

The Sale of Goods Act 1979 provides, in s.29(2), that the place of delivery of the goods is the seller's place of business unless the contract makes a contrary intention clear. In fact, in modern trading, there will frequently be a contrary intention since in most instances the purchaser will want the seller to deliver the goods. The obligation to deliver is discharged by the seller if they deliver the goods at the buyer's premises without negligence to a person apparently having authority to receive them.

It is also provided in the Act that delivery to a carrier is presumed to be delivery to the purchaser. However, this will be so only if the seller has made a reasonable contract of carriage with the carrier. In the case of *Thomas Young & Sons* v. *Hobson and Partners* (1949), electric engines were sent by rail insecurely fixed at the owner's risk. The purchaser was held entitled to reject the goods since they should have been sent at the carrier's risk.

TIME FOR COMPLETION

In a contract for building or engineering works, time is not of the essence unless the contract so provides. In a contract for the sale of goods, time will generally be regarded as of the essence unless the contract provides to the contrary. The significance of time being of the essence is that even if the supplier is late by a single day, then the purchaser will be able to reject the goods and claim damages. If time is not of the essence, then the purchaser's only remedy will be in damages.

It is normal to provide that the supplier or contractor is entitled to an extension of the time for completion if they were delayed by an act or default of the purchaser or by other mitigating circumstances. However, it is to the purchaser's advantage if these circumstances are restricted to ones which are genuinely totally beyond the control of the supplier or contractor. It is also suggested that the circumstances which would justify a claim for an extension should be identified specifically. The use of wide-ranging phrases such as 'any cause beyond the contractor's reasonable control' can lead to problems. In *Scott Lithgow* v. *Secretary of Defence* (1989), a clause reading 'any other cause beyond the contractor's control' was held to include delays due to manufacturing problems in a subcontractor's works. One phrase which should be avoided unless defined is *force majeure* which has no definite meaning in English law.

DAMAGES

The object of an award in damages is to place the injured party in the same financial position as they would have been had the contract been performed properly, provided that the losses are not too remote.

Essentially the rule on remoteness is that the type of loss or damage which is recoverable is that which the parties could reasonably have contemplated at the time when the contract was concluded would be not unlikely to follow from the breach in question. A loss of a particular type could reasonably have been contemplated either because it would arise naturally in the ordinary course of events as a result of the breach or because it should have been contemplated from the particular facts known to the parties at the time of contracting. A supplier of machinery required for production would be taken to know that in the ordinary course of events, a purchaser would suffer a normal loss of profits if delivery were to be delayed. But they would only be liable for profits substantially above the normal level if at the time of entering into the contract the buyer had made that fact known.

Because of the difficulties and uncertainties surrounding the issue of what damages a purchaser will be entitled to if the works are completed late, the contract will often specify the damages which can be recovered per day or week of delay generally up to a maximum. In commercial practice such a clause is often referred to as a penalty clause, but in law there is a sharp distinction between liquidated damages and a penalty:

1. Liquidated damages are a genuine pre-estimate of the losses the purchaser reasonably foresees as likely to arise from the delay or, if they consider that amount to be excessive, some lesser sum. If there is a delay, then the

purchaser is entitled to recover the amount included in the contract as liquidated damages regardless of whether they have actually suffered that loss or not. However, they cannot for that breach of contract recover more than the liquidated damages.

2. A penalty is a sum put into the contract which is excessive in relation to any loss which the purchaser could reasonably anticipate they would suffer as a result of the delay. It is there to frighten the contractor into completing on time. If the clause is classified as a penalty, then it is void and the amount is not recoverable in any action by the purchaser before the courts or an arbitrator. However, this does not alter the fact that the contractor is late and in breach of contract and the purchaser can still recover damages under the ordinary rules given above.

Reference is frequently made in a contract that the supplier or contractor is not liable for 'consequential damages'. It is not clear what that expression covers. Suppliers often think it refers to any loss of profit, but this is not true. In a recent case, it was decided that consequential damages were damages other than those resulting directly and naturally from the breach of the contract. What arises directly and naturally can obviously include a loss of profits. If a supplier or contractor wants to place a limit on their liability for damages, they must use much wider wording such as 'any loss of profit, loss of use, loss of production, loss of contract or any financial or economic loss or for any direct or consequential damage whatsoever'. The only problem then is whether or not such wording would pass the test of reasonableness under the Unfair Contract Terms Act 1977 (see page 78).

QUALITY AND PERFORMANCE

Note that all these obligations are strict, they do not depend on proof of negligence, nor can the seller escape liability by showing that they took all proper steps to ensure goods were of the right quality or that they were not personally to blame.

1. *Description*   Under the Sale of Goods Act 1979, s.13, in a sale by description there is an implied condition that the goods will correspond to the description. For a contract to be classified as a sale by description, then it must have been within the reasonable contemplation of the parties that the purchaser was relying on the description in making the decision to purchase so that the description becomes an essential term of the contract.

2. *Satisfactory quality*   Where a seller sells goods in the course of business there is an implied condition under the Sale of Goods Act 1979, s.14(2), as

amended by the Sale of Goods Amendment Act 1994, that the goods will be of satisfactory quality. This term replaces the old one of merchantable quality. This term does not apply to anything making the goods unsatisfactory which was specifically drawn to the buyer's attention before the contract was made or where the buyer examines the goods before contract and which such examination should have revealed. For the purpose of the Act goods are of satisfactory quality if they meet a standard which a reasonable person would find satisfactory taking into account any description of the goods, the price and other relevant circumstances. The following are stated to be aspects of the quality of the goods:

- fitness for all purposes for which goods of the kind in question are commonly supplied;
- appearance and finish;
- freedom from minor defects;
- safety;
- durability.

3. *Fitness for purpose* While s.14(2) is concerned with fitness for purpose for all purposes for which the goods in question are commonly sold, s.14(3) deals with the position where the buyer has some particular purpose in mind which may not be a purpose for which the goods are commonly sold. It does provide that if the buyer makes it clear to the seller the particular purpose for which the goods are required, either expressly or by implication, then there is an implied condition that they are fit for that purpose. This subsection is narrower than s.14(2), satisfactory quality, in that it requires the buyer to have relied on the seller's skill and judgement. On the other hand, it is wider, in that the goods may in fact be of satisfactory quality but not fit for that particular and uncommon purpose which the buyer made known to the seller. So goods may be perfectly suitable for all destinations in the world to which they are commonly sent, but be unsuitable for some particular destination where there are very extreme weather conditions and the goods may be left exposed in the open. In those circumstances, a buyer would only be likely to succeed in an action against a supplier if they had made known in advance the conditions for which the goods were required, so the seller would have known to supply goods suitable for that purpose. In the case of *Aswan Engineering Industry* v. *Lupdine Ltd* (1987), pails were stacked in the open on the dockside in Kuwait in a temperature of up to 70 °C and no notice given to the supplier. It was held that there was no breach of merchantable quality and no breach of fitness for purpose under s.14(3). Although the case was decided before the revision to the Sale of Goods Act, it is considered that the decision would still be the same under the new definition of satisfactory quality.

PAYMENT

Unless the parties otherwise agree, time of payment is not of the essence of a contract either for the sale of goods or for work and materials. Delays in interim payments by the buyer do not therefore give the seller or contractor the right to terminate or at common law to suspend performance of a contract. Nor was there any right of the seller to be paid interest, until the Late Payment of Commercial Debts (Interest) Act 1998 came into effect for contracts entered into after 1 November 1998. At present, the Late Payment Act only applies where the contract is between a small business, that is one employing less than 50 persons, and either a UK public authority or a large business employer, that is one employing over 50 persons. It is expected that the Act will be made applicable to contracts between two small businesses in two years from the end of 1998 and between all businesses two years later. The contracts covered by the Act are those for the supply of goods and services, and so include standard forms of contract for building and engineering projects. Broadly the effect of the Act is that where it applies there is a statutory right of interest of 8 per cent above bank rate if payment is delayed beyond the date for payment specified in the contract. If no date is specified, then the date used is 30 days from the date of performance of the obligation to which the debt relates. The right of statutory interest may only validly be excluded if there is a substantial contractual remedy for late payment.

With all but very major contracts for the supply of goods, payment is made by the buyer in full after the goods have been accepted. For contracts for construction work and for most contracts for services, it is the general practice that stage payments are made as the work proceeds. The Housing Grants, Construction and Regeneration Act (the Construction Act) now provides a statutory right to stage payments for all construction contracts to which the Act applies and which extend more than 45 days. A construction contract is basically any contract for building or civil engineering work or the provision of architectural or other similar professional services in connection with such contracts. There is no lower limit to the value of the contracts covered by the Act, but there are excluded contracts with a residential occupier for the house which he or she occupies or intends to occupy. Under the Act there must now be a right to stage payments, an adequate mechanism for determining what payments are due under the contract and a final date for payment. Only if a notice satisfying the provisions of the Act has been given can payment be withheld after the final date for payment. The Construction Act also for the first time gives a statutory right under certain circumstances to suspend performance. If a sum due is not paid in full by the due date and no effective notice to withhold payment has been given, then after seven days' notice the party to whom payment should have been made may suspend performance for so long as payment in full is not made.

Also outlawed under the Act are 'pay-when-paid' clauses, that is commonly used clauses under which the contractor only undertakes to pay their subcontractors when they themselves are paid by the client. Now such clauses will only be valid when the person who pays the person due to pay, in the above example the client, becomes insolvent.

The Act allows for the parties to formulate their own contracts complying at least with the Act, but provides that if they fail to do so, then the Scheme for Construction Contracts, SI 1998 No. 649, will apply. There are even more important provisions in the Act relating to the use of adjudication to resolve disputes which are dealt with in Chapter 9.

GUARANTEES AND EXCLUSION CLAUSES

For commercial reasons it has long been the practice of suppliers and contractors to limit their liability in damages for the supply of defective goods and the carrying out of defective work. Often such exclusion clauses are to be found in clauses headed 'Guarantee'. The supplier or contractor usually offers to repair defects arising within a limited period of time from delivery or completion. However, they exclude all liability for breach of any express contractual terms or those implied by law as to the quality or fitness for purpose of the work or for any other breach of their obligations. With contracts between businesses, such clauses fall under the Unfair Contract Terms Act 1977. Despite its title, the Act only deals with terms that seek to limit or exclude liability. The Act is complex but broadly its main provisions provide for the following:

1. Liability for death or personal injury cannot be excluded or restricted by any contract term.
2. A contract term by reference to which a person seeks to exclude or restrict his or her liability for negligence giving rise to any other loss or damage is only valid to the extent to which it passes the test of reasonableness.
3. The implied statutory terms which relate to the description, quality or fitness for purpose of the goods/work in any contract for the supply of goods, hire or work and materials can only be validly excluded or restricted if the clause so doing satisfies the test of reasonableness.
4. Where the contract is on a party's standard terms of contract, then he or she cannot:
   - when in breach of contract exclude or limit his or her liability for that breach of contract; or

- claim to render a contractual performance substantially different from that to be expected or in respect of the whole or any of contractual obligations render no performance at all, unless the contract term satisfied the test of reasonableness.

THE TEST OF REASONABLENESS

The onus or burden of proof is on the person seeking to rely on the clause to show that it is reasonable having regard to what was known or ought to have been known to the parties at the time of contract. The Act lays down certain guidelines to be taken into account in determining whether the test of reasonableness has been satisfied or not, of which the following are most important:

1. The strength of the bargaining position of the parties one to another.
2. Whether the purchaser received an inducement to agree to the term or could have contracted with someone else without such a term.
3. Whether the purchaser knew or ought reasonably to have known of the existence and extent of the term.

In addition, if the clause restricts the liability to a specified sum, then two other guidelines become relevant:

- The resources available to the supplier to meet the liability.
- How far it was open to the supplier to cover himself by insurance.

It now seems clear that the resources available to the supplier will include those of the group to which they belong.

There have now been many cases under the Act but each is very much a decision on its own facts. It has generally been held that in a contract between two business organizations of similar bargaining power, the parties should be left free to apportion risks as they think fit, especially when the risk is insurable. However, it now seems clear that a clause will not satisfy the test of reasonableness if it deprives the purchaser of the implied conditions under the Sale of Goods Act to quality and fitness for purpose, unless the purchaser is given substantial rights to have defects made good. Also an exclusion clause which seeks to deprive the purchaser of the benefit of specific terms in the specification relating to the performance of the goods is also likely to fail the test of reasonableness (*Edmund Murray* v. *BSP International Foundations Ltd*). It may also be difficult for the seller to exclude the purchaser's rights to recover direct damages suffered as a result of the breach although the restriction of these damages to a limit commensurate with the supplier's insurance cover may be reasonable. Exclusion of consequential damages may also be reasonable but there is now the difficulty of knowing what this expression covers. Much importance would also seem to be attached to the extent to which the seller in the course of the negotiations for the contract showed themself by their conduct to be fair and reasonable.

PROFESSIONAL SERVICES

The professional person rendering a service, such as a doctor, lawyer, engineer, architect or surveyor, is in a different position from a supplier or contractor. His or her duty is to exercise the reasonable skill and care to be expected of an ordinarily competent member of that profession. Unless the terms of the contract provide otherwise, and they only very rarely do, the professional person does not guarantee the achievement of a result. A term will not be implied into that person's contract to that effect as a matter of law, but only may be so implied in a particular case as a matter of fact if it is justifiable to do so in all the circumstances.

6 Partnering, benchmarking and incentive contracts

Denise Bower and Fotis Skountzos

The 1990s were characterized by a need to seek new strategies to lower costs and to gain competitive advantage. This chapter discusses how the construction industry uses partnering, benchmarking and incentive contracts to improve its efficiency and provide customer satisfaction. Partnering is an approach to conducting business in an environment where attitudes are changing rapidly. It is the affirmation by all in the construction process that they want to work together. It should not be seen as a cosy arrangement. Benchmarking can assist performance improvement in partnering arrangements and thereby deliver additional benefits. This chapter also identifies the importance of motivation through the application of incentive schemes as a tool to stretch the standards in the construction industry. Even though incentives are not unique in partnering arrangements, they are used to reinforce the behaviour expectations and promote a more proactive, cooperative relationship between the parties.

BACKGROUND

Relationships in the construction industry have always tended to be adversarial, with the parties resorting to contractual claims and litigation, which lengthen timescales and increase costs. These adversarial relationships and the industry fragmentation were identified by the Latham Report (1994) as major barriers to improving quality and productivity. The modern competitive environment has led to an increased need for enhanced productivity and reduced cost. Partnering as a construction method aims to remove the traditional barriers between client and contractor and provide the framework which will ensure that all who are involved in the project understand their objectives and are working towards the same end.

In the early twenty-first century, organizations must gain a competitive edge both domestically and internationally. The modern business environment and intense global competition have created the need for organizations to compare themselves with the best in the world, learn from them and try to overtake them. As a result of this, there have been many initiatives encouraging improvement in various sectors within the construction industry, which has practised benchmarking as a technique for continuous improvement to enhance achievements in areas such as cost reduction, timely delivery and safety. In a partnering arrangement benchmarking can assist performance improvements and establish a continuous improvement philosophy.

The acknowledgement of the important role of motivation and its influence on project success has led to the increased use of incentive schemes in contracts. Incentives are used as a tool to align the project objectives of the client and contractor and not just to motivate the contractor. It is of great importance that incentives for all participants link their performance to the project objectives. Incentives are a key element of achieving commonality in partnering.

PARTNERING

Contracting in the construction industry is very competitive and highly risky. In many instances the perception of conflicting objectives among the parties involved in a construction project leads to adversarial, confrontational and unrewarding relationships (Associated General Contractors of America 1991). The application of the concept of partnering came into existence in the US construction industry in the early 1980s as an effort to improve the relationships between the different parties involved in the construction process. Partnering plays a key role in attaining continuous improvement in design and delivery of construction projects, with latest reports suggesting that cost savings of 40 per cent can be achieved. It has encouraged parties to the construction process to solve problems and eliminate waste, thus promising to change the adversarial culture of the industry. The partnering approach relies on the idea that the best conflict resolution strategy is one that prevents conflicts from occurring. Therefore the main objective of partnering is to encourage all parties to a contract to change their relationship from adversarial to cooperative. This change in relationships requires changes in attitudes to achieve mutual trust, respect and open communication among all parties involved (Abudayyeh 1994).

BASICS OF PARTNERING

The Construction Industry Institute defines partnering as:

a long-term commitment between two or more organisations in achieving common project objectives by maximising resource effectiveness.

(CII 1991)

The key elements are trust, long-term commitment and shared vision. In partnering, trust develops confidence and encourages open communication, exchange of ideas and sharing of resources. Long-term commitment allows constant improvement of technology and methods, reinforces the mutuality of the parties, reduces the rivalry of the traditional contracting system, reduces the attractiveness of litigation and introduces feelings of camaraderie among the parties. Shared vision is the set of common project objectives, formed by consensus through open expectations and established within a candid environment (CII 1991; Crowley and Karim 1995). Partnering is primarily an attitude adjustment where the parties to the contract form a relationship of teamwork, cooperation and good faith performance. The parties are required to look beyond the strict bounds of the contract to develop this cooperative working relationship which promotes their common goals and objectives.

Partnering has been defined in many ways:

> Partnering is a new word for being reasonable, conscientious, and professional. For those who have always kept their goals in sight it is not new, it is just effective project management.
>
> (Larson 1995)

> Partnering is a synergy – a co-operative, collaborative management effort among contracting and related parties to complete a project in the most efficient, cost-effective method possible, by setting common goals, keeping lines of communication open, and solving problems together as they arise.
>
> (American Arbitration Association 1993)

> [Construction partnering means] developing a co-operative management team with key players from the organization involved in a construction contract. The team focuses on common goals and benefits to be achieved through contract execution and develops processes to keep the team working towards those goals. Partnering means exercising leadership for the entire engineering team.
>
> (US Army Corps of Engineers 1991)

> Partnering is a management approach used by two or more organisations to achieve specific business objectives by maximising the effectiveness of each participant's resources. The approach is based on mutual objectives, an agreed method of problem resolution and an active search for continuous measurable improvements.
>
> (Bennet and Jayes 1995)

Partnering can therefore be simply defined as a relationship in which (Cook and Hancher 1990):

- all seek win–win solutions;
- value is placed in long-term relationships;
- trust and openness are norms;
- an environment for profit exists;
- all are encouraged to openly address any problem;
- all understand that neither benefits from exploitation of the other;
- innovation is encouraged;
- each party is aware of the other's needs, concerns and objectives, and is interested in helping their partner achieve them.

It is also important to be aware of what partnering is not (CIB 1997):

Partnering is not a new buzz word for marketers to bandy about to make the same old product more saleable. It also is not:

- A new form of construction contract – it is a procedure for making relationships work better
- An excuse for not working hard to get the best from suppliers and customers
- A soft option
- A quick fix for a weak business – strong players make each other stronger, weak ones destroy each other
- Only about systems and methods – it is about people, enabling them to operate more effectively and efficiently.

FORMS OF PARTNERING

Partnering can be based on a single project (project specific partnering) or on a long-term commitment (strategic partnering). Both project specific and strategic partnering can play a significant role in moving the construction industry away from the traditional adversarial approach.

Project specific partnering is defined as:

a method of applying project specific management in the planning, design and construction profession without the need for unnecessary, excessive, and/or debilitating external party involvement.

(Stephenson 1996)

Strategic partnering is defined as:

a formal partnering relationship that is designed to enhance the success of multiproject experiences on a long-term basis. Just as each individual project must be maintained, a strategic partnership must also be maintained by a periodic review of all projects currently being performed.

(Stephenson 1996)

Project specific partnering suggests a project is entered into with specific sets of objectives which may not be adaptable to a long-term commitment. The main concern for project specific partnering is the time available to set all the essential features in place, and still manage to maintain a successful project. One of the benefits of a project specific partnership is that it has greater long-term significance than strategic partnering for several reasons:

- It does not restrict market entry.
- Price features and improvements are easier to monitor in the relationship.
- Stimulation for competition still exists.

Dedication at the highest levels will have to embrace the project specific partnering philosophy sufficiently to make it work. The mechanisms of joint workshops and facilitators obviously have an influence on the partnering process and the cooperation of participants should allow partnering to generate its own momentum. The challenge of project specific partnering is to allow the benefits available from a strategic partnering arrangement to operate without adversarial relationships developing.

Strategic partnering provides increasing benefits from the lessons learnt on earlier partnered projects. It involves the development of a broader framework focusing on long-term issues, therefore the benefits and problems will be extended to another project to enhance success. Strategic partnering can be used to deal with a planned increase in construction activity that a client is unable to handle with existing staff. It is sensible to start a strategic partnering arrangement by identifying and ranking market sectors in terms of their suitability for partnering. In identifying a market that could provide a basis for partnering, it is important to consider the following recommendations (Hensey 1997):

- Establish a benchmark of performance in the market.
- Define criteria for acceptance or rejection of the potential partner's performance.
- Chart a clear plan for further performance improvements as the partnering arrangement develops.

KEY ELEMENTS OF PARTNERING

It has been suggested that the essence of partnering is the recognition of common goals and the creation of an atmosphere of trust, teamwork and goodwill, which will facilitate the achievement of these goals. The European Construction Institute (ECI) classifies the key elements of successful partnering in two categories: the attitudinal factors and the techniques and procedures of partnering (Scott 2001). The two elements of the latter category will be examined through the partnering process, as they represent well-tried and successful practices for achieving harmonious working relationships and can be applied advantageously, with greater or lesser formality, to projects of all sizes. Together they constitute the structured management framework of partnering (ECI 1997). The attitudinal factors include commitment, trust, development of mutual goals and objectives, and a change of culture.

Commitment

The most important element in establishing a partnering relationship is commitment. Commitment of all parties, as well as everyone with a stake in the relationship, to the shared vision and goals of the project begins with top management and is built into all levels of the project team. Much dedication and hard work by all management levels will be needed to change the traditional adversarial manner of the construction industry. Periodic meetings will ensure the continued commitment of stakeholders, introduce new participants to the partnering process and reinforce team goals. A long-term relationship creates an atmosphere in which companies can achieve a competitive advantage by addressing problems in areas that require constant improvement or extensive time to solve.

Trust

Partnering is founded on trust. Teamwork is not possible if there is cynicism about others' motives. There is better understanding through the development of personal relationships and communication of the goals and the risks undertaken by each stakeholder. With understanding comes trust, and with trust comes the possibility for a synergistic relationship. The partners must recognize that by sharing information, accepting diminished control of a part of its operations and tolerating contact with outsiders, each firm can obtain benefits that would exceed the firm's individual capability. Trust serves to combine the resources and knowledge of the partners in a fashion intended to eliminate adversarial relationships.

Mutual goals and objectives

A fundamental requirement of partnering is to agree mutual goals and objectives. Their role is to ensure that everyone's best interest will be served by concentrating on the success of the project as a whole. Bennet and Jayes (1995) suggest that issues such as improved efficiency, cost reduction, guaranteed profits, fast construction, shared risks, reliable flow of design information and lower legal costs, to quote a few, may be included in the mutually agreed objectives. In finding common ground, the parties soon realize that 'they are in this together' and that success is dependent upon their commitment and ability to work as a team.

Culture

A crucial issue in any partnering arrangement is the attitude of the various parties. Traditional adversarial attitudes do not work, and hence the need for a change in culture. At the outset of the relationship, the parties must have the fundamental belief that they are embarking on a project of mutual benefits, with common goals and objectives. A shift from the 'win–lose' strategy to a 'win–win' plan is imperative. Successful partnering is based on principle-centred working relationships among stakeholders and not on contractual, legal-based relationships.

The partnership cannot run itself, no matter how strong the commitment of management and the participants. It is widely supported that a partnering champion should be appointed at an early stage to promote the partnering concept and culture to the organization, and maintain them throughout the life of the project. The champion will provide the administrative and logistical support that is required to make the partnering agreement work. His or her activities will include scheduling and arranging follow-up meetings, distributing information to all parties and follow-up of procedures and plans developed in partnering meetings. Since partnering promotes success in achieving goals that are of paramount interest to the project manager – quality, cost management, safety and profit, to name a few – he or she would be the logical choice for champion. However, a vital point to remember is that it takes the entire team to make it work.

Partnering is not appropriate on all projects, nor is the size of the project the sole criterion for deciding to partner. The parties that consider embarking on a partnering relationship should identify the sources of risk associated with the project and assess which party is most capable of managing them. It should be accepted that every party is entitled to make a profit and that risks and rewards must be shared fairly. The parties should also be prepared to commit themselves to the partnering principles. It should be kept in mind throughout the process that the focus of partnering is to build cooperative relationships, avoid or minimize disputes and actively pursue the attainment of common goals by the contracting parties.

Following the decision to try partnering on a particular project or contract, and having completed the process designed to provide an environment for developing the cooperative attitude and commitment, the next step is to select the partners. Although the basic principles may be the same, different procedures are applied for the private and public sector clients. In its most effective form partnering will encompass the entire supply chain, including clients, contractors, subcontractors and suppliers in the relationship. The process of selection of partners applies equally to any of the relationships in this chain. The selection is based more on soft issues, such as the parties' understanding and views of partnering, the relevant experience, the resources to be allocated to the project, their management experience and the quality procedures. ECI's *Partnering in the Public Sector* (1997) introduces a five-step selection process:

1. Brief contractors on commitment to partner.
2. Advertise the intention of the client, including the intent to partner.
3. Pre-qualify potential tenderers.
4. Award contract to successful tenderers.
5. Debrief successful tenderers.

It is best to initiate the partnering process as quickly as possible and start aligning objectives, creating trust and establishing teamwork among all those concerned with the project. The workshop is a vital tool for any partnering project. The workshop should be run by an independent facilitator and held at a neutral location. The substance and successful outcome of the workshop are far more important than the mechanics of conducting it. Issues to be addressed during the workshop include the following (Harback, Basham and Buhts 1994):

1. Communication guidelines and ground rules.
2. General partnering concepts.
3. An understanding of conflict and conflict management.
4. Choice of a partnership name.
5. Improvement of team communications.
6. Development of a mission statement.
7. Team discussion and quality indicators.
8. Development of partnership goals.
9. Stages of team evolution.
10. Follow-on task for the partnership.
11. The partnering charter.

The initial workshop should be followed by regular reviews and follow-up workshops to assess the progress of the partnership, keep the parties focused and ensure that the actions taken are consistent with the charter objectives.

The partnering charter is the threshold document in which the parties set forth their mission statement, mutual goals and objectives, and commitment to the partnering relationship. There is no single approach to drafting a partnering charter. The charter should include a mission statement expressing the partners' commitment and agreement to communicate openly and to share information in order to avoid surprises. The partnering charter should also include specific, identifiable goals and objectives, such as:

- delivering the product or service ahead of schedule;
- identifying problems at the first opportunity;
- jointly resolving problems at the lowest possible level;
- seeking fair treatment for all participants;
- limiting cost growth;
- eliminating litigation through the use of alternative dispute resolution (ADR) procedures.

When the parties have established their goals and objectives, they must ensure that they are mutually agreed upon, so that everyone will be actively focused on achieving them. The charter is drawn up during the initial workshop by the participants with the assistance of the facilitator. It must be signed by all the participants in the workshop. Copies of the charter are to be displayed in head and site offices.

The facilitators are not members of the technical or managerial group. They are independent and objective individuals, skilled in team building and group dynamics. They manage the process of the meetings, and not what is decided. Their attention is focused on how decisions are made. Sometimes they may serve to gather information for all team members to support the decision-making process. Above all, the facilitators must remain neutral on the subject under discussion, and their goal is to assist the team in reaching consensus.

The aim of the monitoring process is to ensure that the objectives set out in the partnering charter remain on track. The monitoring criteria, established at the initial partnering workshop, relate both to relationships and to project performance. Performance evaluation reports are normally made monthly, by individual members of the client and contractor organization appointed either at or immediately after the initial workshop. In general, the performance evaluation procedures help to remedy problems that have occurred on the project because of delays in getting the process started.

Continuous improvement should be the prime concern of all parties involved in the project, since without a commitment to it the full range of benefits from partnering will not be realized. Continuous improvement is not possible without benchmarking. Any improvements made to a process should be developed and approved by both parties, and be beneficial to both parties. The continuous improvement process should start at the lowest level possible within the contract and should involve the people who are going to be directly affected by the area of improvement. Furthermore, it should operate in a similar way to quality circles. By continually reviewing the performance of all parties against set objectives it is possible to see an improvement in the project in terms of quality, productivity gains, increased efficiency and staff development.

If an atmosphere of 'trust, dedication to common goals and an understanding of each other's expectations and values' is to be maintained, potential disputes must be addressed quickly, effectively and at the lowest possible level. A ladder of dispute (see Chapter 1) resolution should be established, with dispute identification and resolution being taken care of by the parties at an operational level where possible. Only where internal resolution has failed, or will do greater harm than good, should the parties look towards the external dispute resolution methods advocated by the Latham Report (1994). Resolving disputes at the lowest level reduces the number of escalated disputes that must be resolved by management and, consequently, reduces unwanted strain in the relationship. At the initial workshop a dispute escalation ladder is usually set up. The non-contractual dispute resolution procedure should be agreed post-contract at the initial workshop and incorporated into the partnering arrangement.

Julia Pokora and Colin Hastings (reported by Charlett 1996) identified nine key building blocks for creating effective partnership performance:

1. *Effective screening for fit* There should be compatibility between organizations if they are to work together. There may be problems where the history, culture, values, management style and systems of the partners are not compatible.
2. *The right contractual foundation* A contractual base, which encourages joint problem-solving, information-sharing and risk-taking, should be sought. There should be a move away from an adversarial approach to working and a move towards joint incentives to minimize costs and maximize performance.
3. *Agreeing what the stakeholders want* Different stakeholders have different priorities and success criteria. Stakeholders should be encouraged to be explicit about what is important to them and ways should be devised for exploring and resolving differences in the spirit of problem-solving, rather than attempting to avoid or minimize potential areas of conflict.
4. *Team start-up and team building* Personal relationships and shared understanding can be developed through team start-up workshops.
5. *Making visible different capabilities* Partners should exchange knowledge and experience in a mutually advantageous way. It therefore needs to be established what knowledge and experience each organization has for exchange.
6. *Joint scoping* The client and key parties must work together in defining the scope and specification of the project. There must be a determination to reach a commonly understood and agreed view of what is to be done and how it is to be done.

7. *Partnership information and communication systems* Compatibility of information and communication systems of each participating organization needs to be ensured.

8. *Ground rules for cooperation* There must be a charter or agreement which summarizes the expectations of each party and outlines their aspirations for how they want to work, the behaviours expected of people and the practical methodologies used to achieve this.

9. *Learning review and dissemination* Where the relationship is to endure beyond the initial project, there will be a period of evolution in an innovative way. Attention needs to be paid to the learning process and systems established for reviewing this learning process. Where good practice is established, it may be beneficial to disseminate it to others.

BENEFITS OF PARTNERING

For all the stakeholders of a project, partnering is a high-leveraged effort. It may require increased staff and management time up front, but the benefits accrue in a more harmonious, less confrontational process, resulting in a successful project, without litigation and claims. The partnering process empowers the project personnel and all stakeholders with the freedom and authority to accept responsibility and do their jobs by encouraging decision-making and problem-solving at the lowest possible level of authority.

Substantial benefits can be gained by all members of a project who embrace the partnering concept. For the design professional these might include a reduced exposure to construction claims, a reduction in the shifting of risks inherent in design and construction, an enhanced role in providing design and construction phase services, and a restoration of the ability to provide interpretations of design intent and solutions to problems. Design professionals should expect decreased operational expenses because of the reduction in time and cost spent defending claims and meritless demands, and in preparing to participate in contractor and owner litigation. Finally, they should expect an increased opportunity for successful project completion because of the non-adversarial climate.

Although there is continued room for further refinement, the results so far have been very encouraging. There are many benefits of the partnering process (Baden Hellard 1995; Cook and Hancher 1990; Busch and Pinnell 1994; Stephenson 1996; Larson 1995; Weston and Gibson 1993). This section briefly describes those most noticeable to all parties involved.

Mutual benefits

- Lower risk of time and cost overruns as the contractor and client are working together to complete the project.
- Completion on time.
- Reduced exposure to litigation – efficient resolution of problems.
- Less confrontation through informal conflict management procedures. The sharing of information and the environment of trust contribute to the swift solving of problems, before they escalate to disputes.
- Avoidance of litigation through a jointly developed dispute resolution mechanism.
- Improved performance and project quality. There is a higher quality because energies are focused on the ultimate goal of construction and not misdirected to adversarial concerns.
- Early anticipation and resolution of problems. The partners proactively anticipate problems and design an action plan addressing how those problems will be jointly resolved or avoided. They recognize problems will occur during contract performance and that the existence of these problems does not mean that their relationship has failed.
- Reduced administration and oversight. With increased communication and empowerment by senior management, partners find a significant reduction in the need for layers of administration. Furthermore, a reduction in administration costs has been observed.
- Reduced time and cost of contract performance. By establishing open communication as a guiding principle, parties to partnering arrangements have found that issues are raised more expeditiously. This enables the partners to meet or exceed contractual schedule requirements and avoid costly mistakes or rework.
- Increased innovation through open communication and trust, especially in the development of value engineering, changes and constructability improvements.
- Increased opportunity for a financially successful project because of the non-adversarial, 'win–win' attitude.
- Buildable designs.
- Improved safety. Taking joint responsibility for ensuring a safe work environment for contractor and client employees reduces the risk of hazardous work conditions and avoids workplace accidents.

Benefits to the client

- Reduced cost associated with contractor selection, contract administration, mobilization and the learning curve of beginning a project with a new contractor.

- Reduction in fixed overheads.
- Reduced involvement of senior management in handling adversarial claims.
- Effective utilization of personnel resources.
- Better opportunity for innovation and value engineering.

Benefits to the contractor

- Secured profits and better cash flow, through more realistic pricing and regular payments.
- The long-term, non-adversarial aspects of partnering imply that revenues may be more stable.
- Opportunity to refine and develop new skills in a controlled and low risk environment.
- Optimum use of resources.
- Improved productivity and lower administrative costs, due to focus on the project rather than on case-building.
- Lower overhead costs.

Clients seem to be attracted to partnering due to the growing body of evidence that suggests that partnering can deliver the 30 per cent cost savings advocated by the Latham Report (Hosie 1997). On the other hand, it can be argued that the appeal of partnering to the contractors is that it can offer long-term relationships and more secure profits. However attractive partnering may be to both clients and contractors, there are barriers that may inhibit its successful application.

BARRIERS TO SUCCESSFUL PARTNERING

Partnering represents a significant change in the way projects are managed in the construction industry. Such change is likely to meet resistance. A study by Larson and Drexler (1997) revealed that barriers to successful partnering might stem from five main themes. A summary of their findings is presented below.

Mistrust and interpersonal barriers to cooperation

These barriers include failure to build a true relationship of trust, fear of the unknown and change, differing values and culture, and a lack of understanding of risks and how they are redistributed in a partnering environment. Many people have an instinctive suspicion of the other party due to their past experiences. They are concerned that information divulged could be used against them at a later day. They also cannot admit that there is another way. In summary, it can be said that some people simply cannot accept partnering as a long-term way of doing business.

Nature and structure of projects that inhibit partnering

The main barrier here appears to be related to government and legal issues. Public projects require complete documents and a fixed price, precluding full partnering. The construction industry seems to be too reliant on legal protection. Furthermore, the low bid methods of awarding projects appear to lead to built-in conflict. Other project structure issues identified as barriers include the internal bureaucracy at many companies, difficulty in finding the appropriate partner and the fact that some projects are simply not appropriate for partnering.

Perceptions of the partnering process that discourage partnering

A number of factors associated with the partnering process itself were identified as barriers. The first of these was the perceived lack of common goals among the parties involved in the construction industry. Real-time cost associated with trying to align both organizations with every undertaking was also identified as a barrier. Project planning was claimed to be often inadequate. Finally, partnering costs were seen as too costly in an industry that prides itself on operating 'lean and mean'. The importance of these perceptions increases if one considers that an expected consequence of partnering is cost reduction.

Knowledge and skill barriers

Unfamiliarity with or misunderstanding of partnering concepts were identified as important barriers. Others were the inexperience in this type of approach to contracting, the lack of understanding of the partner companies' culture and 'old-fashioned management'.

Lack of firm commitment to partnering

The level of commitment, or lack thereof, especially from top management, was identified as a barrier.

BENCHMARKING

Benchmarking, in its current form, is derived from the work of Robert Camp in the late 1970s. Essentially it has a number of key characteristics. It is a management tool that has its roots in the business environment. It is used to identify changes needed in products and processes to achieve better company performance. From a comparison of the manufacture of photocopiers in the USA and Japan, Camp (1989, 1995) devised a model of benchmarking supported by a number of steps. It involves analysing an existing situation, identifying and measuring factors critical to the success of the product or process, comparing them with other businesses, analysing the results and implementing an action plan to achieve better performance. Since then a number of models and processes have been developed and applied across a broad range of subject areas (Pickrell and Garnett 1996).

Benchmarking definitions have mainly been derived from experiences in manufacturing. There are slight deviations in definitions, depending on the focus and scope of application. According to Camp (1989), 'Benchmarking is the search for industry best practices that lead to superior performance'. In this definition the author portrays a very generalized view of benchmarking. The focus is on adopting the best practices or methods to achieve superior performance. The definition implies that the best practices are to be pursued, regardless of where they exist.

BENCHMARKING IN CONSTRUCTION

The focus of benchmarking in manufacturing is the ability to meet customer requirements and to adopt innovative practices regardless of their source. Over the years manufacturing organizations have developed measures to assess their performance. Construction, because of the diversity of its products and processes, is one of the last industries to embrace objective performance measurement. This does not diminish the potential benefits that can be derived. However, benchmarking attempts in construction are bound to face difficulties. The fact that a number of organizations get involved in designing and constructing a single project, and the temporary nature of the construction process, make the benchmarking task a complex one.

Benchmarking only works if consistent methods of measuring the performance of operations can be developed and introduced. Such methods do not exist in the construction industry. That adds to the difficulty in using benchmarking effectively as a basis for comparison. The majority of the relatively limited number of studies devoted to construction productivity and performance measurement is concerned with the identification of sources of delays, rather than with the analysis of measuring systems and techniques (Mohamed 1996).

Benchmarking needs to be tailored to the construction industry. However, there are a number of factors that may hinder its use. First, the nature of the construction industry itself, with its large number of variables, makes a direct comparison difficult. Such variables are location, size and type of project and level of technology. The efficiency of the project team can be further hampered by the diversity in cultural backgrounds of the team. The real difficulty, however, lies in the way in which improvement of the process requires each individual company to change. This may not be reflected in the benefit accrued to that company, although it is possible that a company operating further downstream will reap the rewards from the improvement. There is, therefore, little incentive for resource outlay by one company if the benefit is assigned to another. To some extent, all these problems have been addressed by the manufacturing and service industries. Benchmarking provides a rigorous and tested methodology to facilitate the change process, but it should first be tailored for use in a construction environment (Pickrell and Garnett 1996).

If the construction industry is to manage its affairs successfully, it must have a measurement system to monitor best practices and productivity. Benchmarking is therefore an essential and powerful tool for business improvement. Its adoption by the industry could result in measurable performance improvement, facilitating real cost reduction. Benchmarking is not simply about recording statistical data relevant to construction projects, but is a continuous process of comparing methodologies of the many processes of construction and their resultant effect – both within the industry and outside when possible. By encouraging the industry to share and then to strive to meet or exceed current 'best practice', benchmarking should provide a catalyst for change and improve performance (CIB Working Group 11 1996).

BENCHMARKING AND PARTNERING

A particular strength of benchmarking is that it can be used alongside many other improvement techniques. A recent consideration has been the potential benefits to assist partnering. There are several ways in which benchmarking and partnering link, as in the need for performance measures. Benchmarking can assist performance improvement in partnering arrangements in many ways. Pickrell and Garnett (1996) suggest the following three levels as an example:

1. Within the general business, with benefits assisting partnering arrangements, for example improving data transfer.
2. On a project-to-project basis with partners, increasing the use of standardized products.
3. Between partnering arrangements (as in learning from the positive experiences of other arrangements). It can include different arrangements within the organization, partnering arrangements in different sectors of the same industry and partnering in other industries.

At the moment there are few ways of proving the benefits of partnering in the construction industry. This constitutes one of the main barriers for the use of partnering. Hence, metrics are used to establish an organization's position. Once business leaders have been identified, implementation of their reasons for being better can take place. A criticism of partnering is reduced competition. Benchmarking allows the companies to keep a view on the competition, which can then be fed back into the partnering arrangement (Pickrell and Garnett 1996).

Within the partnering environment, benchmarking becomes a generic and holistic approach to continuous improvement. Therefore it may not be necessary to make comparisons with a world-class and established organization, since it will take a long time to complete a full and incremental step procedure to the benchmarking exercise. Unless the size of the organization has the resources required, it may be impractical to fully implement the findings owing to the size of gap that may be involved. In spite of the criticisms directed against UK companies that do not benchmark against world leaders, the way forward for partnering arrangements is to set incremental steps on a continuous basis, with world-class performance as a long-range goal (NEDO 1993).

Benchmarking should be used to compare with other projects, with a wide range of comparators used to identify where improvements can be made. The achievement of continuous improvement requires individuals and teams who do not idly accept the status quo, but constantly seek opportunities for improvement. It is essential to measure performance in the areas agreed in the workshops at specified intervals and to feed back the results to the project team. Simple measures that could be developed and refined as the project proceeds can be used as a starting point (CIB Working Group 12 1997; CIB 1998). The principles of benchmarking vis-à-vis the effectiveness of the partnering charter being used should be addressed by the group at the workshops. This involves reference to the charter goals and the targets which the group consider necessary to achieve the objectives. These targets are a measure (indicator) of the level of success or failure for each of the goals (CIB Working Group 12 1997).

Benchmarking in partnering can be used as a tool for improvement. The achievement of continuous improvement is a prime motive for partnering. Without a commitment to continuous improvement, the full benefits from partnering will not be realized. Continuous improvement is not possible without benchmarking. Benchmarking best practices is essential for survival at the beginning of the twenty-first century (CIB Working Group 12 1997; NEDO 1993).

INCENTIVES AND PARTNERING

ROLE OF INCENTIVES IN PARTNERING

What attracts contractors to partnering is the better and long-term relationships that the process engenders. Incentives in the form of target costs with shared savings between client and contractor are also an attractive aspect of partnering arrangements. Perhaps the simplest explanation for the growth in popularity of partnering is its ability to realize a basic truth: if the project is completed on time, to a high quality and within budget, then all participants are going to reap financial benefits. Long-term partnering offers its own incentives in the form of a stable workload over an extended period. Incentive payments linked to time, cost, quality or safety are usual. The important distinction between the partnering arrangement and the traditional target cost contract is the emphasis on quality and safety as target factors. What attracts clients to partnering is the growing body of evidence that, as a procurement method, it is better placed to deliver the cost saving of 30 per cent advocated by Latham (1994) (see Hosie 1997).

Clients and contractors are creating partnerships with the aim of achieving the objectives of both parties: higher profit to the contractor at lower cost to the client. The measurement of the performance of the partnership is an important feature of the concept. The main objective is to continually improve the processes and the products. The aim is to ensure that every year produces improved performance. Continuous improvement should be the concern of all the parties involved in the project, as it is only effective when all parties are motivated to its achievement. The end result is a measurable increase in value, whilst properly meeting the client's needs (CIB 1998; Bennet and Jayes 1995).

Incentives are not unique to partnering contracts and are not used universally in partnering relationships. When incentives are used in partnering, they serve to reinforce behaviour expectations, focusing attention on the traditional measures of costs and schedule, and on quality improvement, innovation and interface enhancement. The two categories of incentives are monetary and non-monetary. Monetary incentives include adjustable fee, cash awards if criteria are met, bonus/penalty as percentage of base fee, shared savings on cost-plus-guaranteed-maximum and safety/schedule incentives. Non-monetary incentives are designed to express appreciation for the employees' efforts, resulting in better employee performance (such as gifts, barbecues and partnering newsletters identifying high performers) (CII 1991).

Profit-sharing schemes serve to concentrate everyone's efforts on minimizing the impact of high risk items that occur on a project. Rather than expecting some parties to carry risks, which may or may not occur, it is more efficient for the whole team to have a real incentive to work hard when problems arise and to solve them at the lowest cost. Profit sharing is one way of achieving this change in attitude. The use of profit sharing often gives rise to questions about who provides the extra money that is shared out. Clients sometimes assume they will have to pay more to provide the incentives for everyone else. Bennet and Jayes (1995) suggest that partnering provides extra money from greater efficiency and avoiding wasted effort otherwise used in pursuit of adversarial approaches. In other words, they advocate that partnering, by improving the traditional inefficient approaches, delivers the extra money needed to fund real incentives for the whole project team, including the client. Financial incentives are usually provided through profit sharing. This is especially effective where the criteria used to determine each firm's share are carefully related to the agreed mutual objectives.

An incentive–disincentive payment system can be used as a prevention technique of issue resolution. It involves payment of a bonus, or incentive, to a contract party for performing its work in a superior manner, to the specified quality. The bonus may relate to cost, time, quality, safety or other such measurable components of the total job performance. If the standards set are not achieved by a measurable point of the project, the disincentive clause is triggered and the contract party is penalized for less-than-satisfactory performance on the project. Incentives–disincentives tend to affect the project staff in a manner that is considered by some as threatening and by others as a stimulant to do the work better within the contract specified quality. It is important though to understand that incentives and disincentives do not necessarily resolve issues. They simply encourage, by the promise of reward, prompt resolution of those problems (Stephenson 1996).

Bennet and Jayes (1995) report that partnering is most likely to be successful if the agreed mutual objectives provide a realistic chance that all the parties will earn a fair return. The mutual objectives may include many issues, but common subjects include improved efficiency, cost reduction, guaranteed profits, reliable product quality, certain completion on time, continuity of workload, shared risks, reliable flow of design information and lower legal costs. They suggest that it helps project teams to find good mutual objectives if they are reinforced by well thought out incentive schemes. The success of a partnering relationship will be enhanced by the use of incentive performance schemes (CII 1991).

INCENTIVE SCHEMES AS A MEANS TO STRETCH TARGETS

CII's Partnering Task Force (1991) incorporated shared incentives, as part of the establishment of performance measurement systems and continuous improvement processes, into the partnering implementation process. This

99

involves consideration of an incentive modification to the agreement through which the partners can share costs and rewards associated with improvements, the setting of incentives all the way down to individuals and documenting and communicating early accomplishments.

The incentive performance schemes are tools to measure risks and rewards of the partnership. Performance can be assessed against predefined benchmarks for various classifications of performance indicators. These indicators combine traditional elements such as productivity and man-hour ratios. However, future improvements can only come about by successfully creating a greater 'business focus' with the emphasis on the results, rather than the process. Performance categories may include productivity, performance, safety and environment, and management control. These performance factors are interrelated and inter-dependent.

It is essential to ensure continuous improvement in performance when partnering. Performance should be measured regularly and the results used to set tougher targets for the next period. The improvements achieved each year should be recorded in a report to the main boards of all firms involved in the partnering arrangement to ensure top management's continued commitment. It is important to agree at the outset the most appropriate tools to achieve an objective measurement of performance. Workshops should identify the distinctive improvements that the project intends to make and devise a clear measure of how success will be judged (CIB 1998; Bennet and Jayes 1995).

The benefits and rewards can be achieved through challenging established practice and the search for 'something different'. A tool deployed in this area is the creation of stretch targets on specific deliverables, creating the scenario where existing methods could not possibly yield the target result. Individuals or both teams, contractor and client, should share the benefits from inventiveness. By incentivizing the contract we stretch targets, looking at the standards, which have been identified through benchmarking, to achieve best value for money. Incentivization creates a more proactive, cooperative relationship between the partners.

CONCLUSIONS

PARTNERING

The construction industry has been heavily criticized for its low productivity and poor performance and is under increasing pressure to improve productivity, safety, the quality and value of the final product, and the efficiency and effectiveness of its processes. Partnering has been seen as a project management tool to overcome the traditional obstacles that can adversely impact a successful construction project. Implementing a partnering agreement requires the recognition of common goals by all parties, the creation of an atmosphere of trust and teamwork and commitment to a long-term relationship. We believe that the key elements of partnering highlighted here are crucial to the development of a successful partnering relationship. Despite the fact that partnering is a relatively new concept, it has been used successfully on a number of projects and there are substantial benefits to be gained by all parties from its use. However, barriers to the growth of partnering do exist and may inhibit its successful application. An active partnering process during the preparation of a project can result in significant cost improvement.

BENCHMARKING

The aim of any benchmarking effort is to introduce improvements to better meet customer needs. Various authors have described benchmarking as an improvement process used to discover and incorporate best practices that will lead to superior performance. Benchmarking is based on the philosophy of continuous improvement. A number of factors that may hinder the use of benchmarking in construction have been identified, the main one being the nature of the construction industry itself with its large number of variables that makes direct comparison difficult. Therefore benchmarking should first be tailored for use in the construction environment. One of the main advantages of benchmarking is that it can be used alongside many other improvement techniques. Benchmarking in partnering can be used as a tool for continuous improvement to set targets for incremental steps with world-class performance as a long-range goal.

INCENTIVES

The study of the relevant literature has revealed the important role incentives can play in construction contracts. The contractual relationship between the client and the contractor is a key to project success. Taking advantage of a contractor's general objective to maximize its profits by giving it the opportunity to earn a greater profit if it performs the contract efficiently lies at the core of incentive contracting. Incentivization can create a more cooperative relationship between parties, overcoming the traditional adversarial approach to contracting. It requires, though, time and a clear objective of what is to be achieved. Structuring an effective incentive programme could prove to be a complex undertaking. The purpose of the incentives is not just to motivate the contractor, but to tie performance of all

101

participants to the project's objectives. The proper use of an incentive contract aligns the priorities of project participants who would otherwise have diverse motives.

When incentives are used in a partnering setting, they focus attention not only on the traditional measures of cost and schedule, but also on quality improvements, innovation and interface enhancement. It is of the utmost importance to ensure continuous improvement in performance when partnering. Incentive performance schemes have been used as tools to measure the risks and rewards of the partnership and set tougher targets to achieve for the next period of time.

REFERENCES AND FURTHER READING

Abudayyeh, O. (1994), 'Partnering, a team building team approach to quality construction management', *Journal of Management in Engineering, ASCE,* **10**(6), November/December.

American Arbitration Association (1993), *Construction Industry Dispute Avoidance: The Partnering Process*, American Arbitration Association, NCDRC, New York.

Associated General Contractors of America (AGC) (1991), *Partnering: A Concept for Success*, Associated General Contractors of America, Washington, DC.

Baden Hellard, R. (1995), *Project Partnering: Principle and Practice*, Thomas Telford, London.

Bennet, J. and Jayes, S. (1995), *Trusting the Team: The Best Practice Guide to Partnering in Construction*, Centre for Strategic Studies in Construction, The University of Reading.

Busch, J. S. and Pinnell, S. S. (1994), 'Dispute management programs: partnering, claims management and dispute resolution', in *Proceedings of the Project Management Institute 25th Annual Symposium, Vancouver*, Project Management Institute, Sylva, NC, October.

Camp, R. C. (1989), *Benchmarking: The Search for the Industry Best Practices that lead to Superior Performance*, ASQC Quality Press, Milwaukee, WI.

Camp, R. C. (1995), *Business Process Benchmarking*, ASQC Quality Press, Milwaukee, WI.

Charlett, A. J. (1996), 'A review of partnering arrangements within the construction industry and their influence on performance', in *Proceedings of the International Council for Building Research Studies and Documentation (CIB), W89 Beijing International Conference, Beijing, China*, October. http://www.bre.polyu.edu.hk/careis/rp/cibBeijing96/papers/130_139/138/p 138.htm

Construction Industry Board (CIB) Working Group 11 (1996), *Towards a 30% Productivity Improvement in Construction*, Thomas Telford, London.

Construction Industry Board (CIB) Working Group 12 (1997), *Partnering in the Team*, Thomas Telford, London.

Construction Industry Board (CIB) (1998), 'Fact sheet on benchmarking', Construction Industry Board home page, http://www.ciboard.org.uk/factsht. htm, February.

Construction Industry Institute (CII) Partnering Task Force (1991), 'In search of partnering excellence', *Special Publication No. 17-1*, CII, Austin, TX.

Construction Industry Institute (CII) (1995), 'Use of incentives', *Implementation Status Report, 1995 CII Conference*, CII, Austin, TX.

Construction Industry Institute (CII) Partnering Task Force (1996), 'Model for partnering excellence', *Research Summary No. 102-1*, CII, Austin, TX.

Cook, L. and Hancher, E. (1990), 'Partnering: contracting for the future', *Journal of Management in Engineering, ASCE*, **6**(4), October.

Cook, S. (1995), *Practical Benchmarking*, Kogan Page, London.

Crowley, G. L. and Karim, A. (1995), 'Conceptual model of partnering', *Journal of Management in Engineering, ASCE*, **11**(5), September/October.

European Construction Institute (ECI) (1997), *Partnering in the Public Sector*, ECI, Loughborough.

Harback, H. F., Basham, D. L. and Buhts, R. H. (1994), 'Partnering paradigm', *Journal of Management in Engineering, ASCE*, **10**(1), January/February.

Hensey, M. (1997), 'Strategic planning; development and improvements', *Journal of Management in Engineering, ASCE*, **13**(1).

Hosie, J. (1997), *Partnering – the Next Milestone in Construction Procurement?*, Construction Law Review, London.

Larson, E. (1995), 'Project partnering: results of study of 280 construction projects', *Journal of Management in Engineering, ASCE*, **11**(2), March/April.

Larson, E. and Drexler, J. A. Jr. (1997), 'Barriers to project partnering: report from the firing line', *Project Management Journal*, **28**(1), March.

Latham, Sir Michael (1994), *Constructing the Team: Final Report of the Government/Industry Review of Procurement and Contractual Arrangements in the UK Construction Industry*, The Stationery Office, London, GB, 1994.

Mohamed, S. (1996), 'Benchmarking and improving construction productivity', *Benchmarking for Quality Management and Technology*, **3**(3).

National Economic Development Organisation (1993), *Partnering without Conflict*, NEDO, London.

Pickrell, S. and Garnett, N. (1996), 'Generic benchmarking in construction', in *Proceedings of the International Council for Building Research Studies and*

103

Documentation (CIB), W89 Beijing International Conference, Beijing, China,
October.
http://www.bre.polyu.edu.hk/careis/rp/cibBeijing96/papers/130_139/138/p
138.htm

Scott, R. (ed.) (2001), *Partnering in Europe: Incentive-based alliancing for projects,*
Thomas Telford, London.

Stephenson, R. J. (1996), *Project Partnering for the Design and Construction
Industry,* Wiley, New York.

US Army Corps of Engineers (1991), *Construction Partnering: The Joint Pursuit of
Common Goals to Enhance Engineering Quality,* US Army Corps of Engineers,
Omaha, NB.

Weston, D. C. and Gibson, G. E. Jr. (1993), 'Partnering-project performance in
U.S. Army Corps of Engineers', *Journal of Management in Engineering, ASCE,*
9(4), July/August.

7 Procurement

Peter Baily

Purchasing has been defined as:

> the process by which organizations define their needs for goods and services, identify and compare the suppliers and supplies available to them, negotiate with sources of supply or in some way arrive at agreed terms of trading, make contracts and place orders, and finally receive the goods and services and pay for them.
>
> (Baily 1987)

It is in the details of this process that project purchasing differs from purchasing for batch production or continuous production, rather than in the aims and objectives. The aims and objectives at their most basic are to arrange for the supply of goods and services of the required quality at the time required from satisfactory suppliers at an appropriate price. But to achieve these basic aims, purchasing departments may need to engage in a variety of activities aimed at subsidiary objectives, including purchase research, supplier development, and so on.

Project purchasing has two main subdivisions: buying parts and materials, and placing subcontracts. Closely associated with these buying activities are the related activities of expediting (or progressing), which is intended to ensure delivery on time, and inspection and quality control, which are intended to ensure delivery to specification, together with stores management and stock control.

SOME SPECIAL CHARACTERISTICS OF PROJECT PURCHASING

Differences between project purchasing and purchasing for other operations are most noticeable on large projects. Small projects do not differ much in their purchasing requirements from jobbing production or (if they are undertaken on a regular and frequent basis) batch production. Batch production, with most batch sizes in the 6 to 6000 range, accounts for two-thirds of UK manufacturing output. As far as the printer and binder are concerned, this book is itself part of batch production, although for the editor and publisher it is more an example of project production. Differences exist in:

- the way specifications are arrived at (with a single client playing a dominant role);
- the way suppliers are identified and compared (with the client often involved and sometimes insisting on the use of particular sources of supply);
- the often complicated details of cash flow and payments in and out.

Project production is essentially discontinuous, in comparison with batch production and continuous production. Even though the company concerned may expect to undertake a series of projects of similar type, nevertheless each project stands on its own. It is therefore very important to devise and negotiate terms and conditions of contract which are appropriate for the individual project and which so far as possible cover all eventualities.

Differences also exist in the way the purchasing people, and those on associated activities, are slotted into the organization structure. For large projects, the project manager may have full-time staff, including a purchase manager, attached to the project for several years. Much has been written about matrix organizations, which do not comply with classical organization theories because senior people answer to at least two bosses. The project purchasing manager, for instance, would be responsible both to the project manager and to the purchasing director in the permanent organization structure. He or she would in principle have line responsibility to the senior project manager and functional responsibility to the purchasing director: one would be concerned with *what* is to be done and *when*, while the other would be concerned with *how* it should be done. In practice things are not always quite so clear-cut, which is why people in matrix organization structures have to be able to cope successfully with fluid situations, political pressures, uncertainty and conflicts of interest.

An important responsibility of such a project purchasing chief for a very large project would be manpower planning, which would, of course, be done in consultation with his or her immediate bosses. Some purchasing staff would be seconded to the project for the whole of its duration or at any rate the greater part of it. Others would be attached for a shorter period. It might be necessary to cope with peak workloads by hiring outside personnel on short contracts. At the other extreme, some of the purchasing work could be dealt with no doubt by permanent staff who had not been attached to the project full time, as part of their normal work.

THE PROJECT PURCHASING MANAGER

A sample job description for a project purchasing manager on a very large project taking years to complete is given in Figure 7.1.

1. Reports directly to the project manager and liaises with other managers in the project team.
2. Provides a procurement service to the project manager. This includes subcontracting, ordering equipment and materials, expediting, inspection and shipping.
3. Represents the project manager in meetings with the client on all procurement matters.
4. Prepares procurement procedures for the project in agreement with the project manager, corporate procurement management and the client.
5. Ensures that the project procurement procedures are adhered to.
6. Directly supervises the chief subcontracts buyer, chief buyer, senior project expediter and the senior project purchasing inspector.
7. Reviews and agrees regularly with the project manager and with corporate procurement management the manpower needs of the project procurement department.
8. Maintains close liaison with corporate procurement management on all project procurement activities.
9. Supervises the preparation of:
   - conditions of contract and subcontract;
   - list of approved suppliers and subcontractors;
   - detailed inspection procedures;
   - shipping documentation; and
   - all other documentation required for project procurement.
10. Agrees the names of firms to be invited to tender in conjunction with the client.
11. Attends the opening of tenders when sealed tender procedures apply.
12. Monitors and reviews procurement progress on a continuous basis and prepares monthly status reports. Attends and reports to project progress meetings whenever the progress of purchases and subcontracts is being considered.
13. Signs bid summaries before their submission to the project manager and the client, after ensuring that the correct procedures have been followed.
14. Supervises the placement of all procurement commitments, whether these are by letter of intent, purchase order, contract or any other form.
15. Ensures that copies of purchase orders, correspondence and all relevant documents, including drawings, specifications, test certificates, operating and maintenance manuals, are correctly distributed to the client, the project manager or elsewhere as laid down in the project purchasing procedures.
16. Obtains from suppliers and subcontractors schedules of work compatible with the project programme.
17. Ensures that negotiations concerning orders and subcontracts are properly conducted and takes personal responsibility if they are critical.
18. Ensures that invoice queries from the invoice checking section are promptly dealt with by procurement staff.

Figure 7.1 Sample job description of a project purchasing manager on a very large project

SUBCONTRACTING

Large projects are usually the subject of one main contract between the client (or customer, purchaser or employer if these terms are preferred) and the main contractor. The main contractor will then place a number of subcontracts, which themselves constitute contracts between it and the subcontractors (Chapter 2). The client is not legally a party to these subcontracts, but will usually take part in the process of awarding them, deciding on the subcontractors, approving the terms and conditions, and so on. In effect the client is subcontracting part of its purchasing activity to the main contractor and will naturally want to keep an eye on things (except in turnkey contracts) and perhaps also to stipulate that certain preferred firms should be used as subcontractors. This can be seen from the points 3, 4, 10 and 15 in the project purchasing manager's job description example in Figure 7.1. Computerized databases are increasingly being used to assist in finding possible subcontractors and suppliers.

Suppliers have a long way to go between finding a possible customer and actually getting the business. Quality capability is important. Track record is very important. At the time the British offshore oil and gas industry was getting under way, the government set up the Offshore Supplies Office (OSO). This was established to ensure that available business was not pre-empted by overseas-based organizations which had built up track records in offshore work in South America, North America and other parts of the world to the exclusion of home-based organizations which were trying to break into new market opportunities. A voluntary agreement between the Offshore Supplies Office and the operators included, for example, the following clauses:

1. All potential suppliers selected to bid are given an equal and adequate period in which to tender, such period to take into account the need to meet demonstrably unavoidable critical construction or production schedules of the operator.
2. Any special conditions attached to the materials, the source of supply of components and materials, and the inspection of goods are stated in the specification or enquiry documents.
3. Stated delivery requirements are not more stringent than is necessary to meet the construction and/or production schedules of the operator.
4. Where the requirement includes the need to develop equipment or proposals in conjunction with the operator, all bidders are given equal information at the same time.
5. When the operator is unable to identify a reasonable number of suitably qualified UK suppliers for its invitation to tender, it will consult the OSO before issuing enquiries.

6. The enquiry documents require the potential bidders to estimate the value of the UK content of the goods and/or services to be supplied.
7. When the operator has determined its decision for the award of contract, in the case of non-UK award it will inform the OSO prior to notifying selected suppliers and will give the OSO a reasonable time, in the circumstances applying, for representation and clarification. This procedure will be followed in the case of subcontracts referred by main or subcontractors to the operator for approval. Where the operator does not intend to call for prior approval of subcontracts, the procedure for adherence to the Memorandum of Understanding and this Code of Practice will be agreed between the operator and the OSO. Where this gives the OSO access to the operator's contractors and subcontractors, this procedure will not diminish the direct and normal contractual relationship between the operator and its suppliers. The principle will be adopted that following disclosure of prior information to the OSO on intended awards no subsequent representation to the operator by a potential supplier, other than at the request of the operator, will be entertained.
8. To satisfy the OSO that full and fair opportunity is being given to UK suppliers operators will, on request, make available to officers of the OSO such information as they may reasonably require about:
   ● the programme of intended enquiries to industry necessary to implement the anticipated overall programme of exploration and/or development to the extent that this information has not already been made available to the Department of Energy. (The operators may supply this information in any format convenient to themselves provided it is sufficiently comprehensive to enable the OSO to assess the potential opportunity for UK industry.)

How long such agreements should last, and indeed whether or not there is still any justification for them, are matters outside the scope of this chapter.

THE PURCHASING CYCLE

Conventional notions of the purchasing cycle which apply in batch production, mass production or in merchandising are less appropriate to the realm of the complex project. Large complex projects, such as the construction of complete factories, fully equipped hospitals and offshore oil rigs, are carried out all over the world. Purchase departments are involved on both sides of the contract: on the client's side, in obtaining and helping to analyse tenders and in contract negotiation; and on the contractor's side, in obtaining information from subcontractors and suppliers that is needed in preparing the bid or tender. Once the contract is settled, a large number of orders and subcontracts need to be placed by the contractor's purchase department, usually with the approval of the client.

It is often desirable to use the expert knowledge and experience of contractors in converting the preliminary functional specification into the final build specification. Two-stage tendering is sometimes used for this purpose. There are several versions of this. The World Bank, in its booklet *Guidelines for Procurement under World Bank Loans*, suggests that the first stage could be to invite unpriced technical bids. Based on these, a technical specification would be prepared and used for the second stage, in which complete priced bids are invited.

It is difficult to reconcile the public accountability requirement that all tenderers have equality of information and are bidding for the same specification with the common-sense purchasing principle that exceptional expertise on the part of a supplier should be used in preparing the specification. To expect a contractor with unique design and construction ability to tell the client the best way to do a job, without payment, and then in the second stage to lose the contract to a low bidder with less design capability, seems unlikely to work out. Such firms sometimes insist on some version of the cost-plus contract or on negotiated contracts.

Once the contract has been signed, purchasing work goes ahead on placing the subcontracts. Very often this has to be done in conjunction with the client, as shown in Figure 7.2. Specifications are prepared, possibly in consultation with vendors and incorporated in the Request for Quotation documents. Normal practice is to allow a month for quotations to be submitted, although on bigger subcontracts running into millions of pounds' worth of work more time may be necessary. Further discussion with suppliers may take place after receipt of tenders, to clarify matters, before the bid analysis is prepared for discussion with the client.

An example of a bid analysis form is shown in Figure 7.3. This provides columns in which to list the bids received, allowing comparisons with budget, freight and duty, escalation and other extras. The form also includes a questionnaire on the vendor selected, in which explicit reference must be made to its past record, experience, shop facilities, test equipment and other important aspects of vendor selection.

Whatever procedure is adopted, it is unusual for a bid for a major subcontract to be accepted exactly as made, despite the parity of tender principle. Several meetings between the buyer and the preferred bidder (or bidders) may be required to negotiate aspects of the specification and commercial terms and conditions. After all bids have been received and appraised, with perhaps only one bidder still in the running, detailed negotiations still continue to establish identity

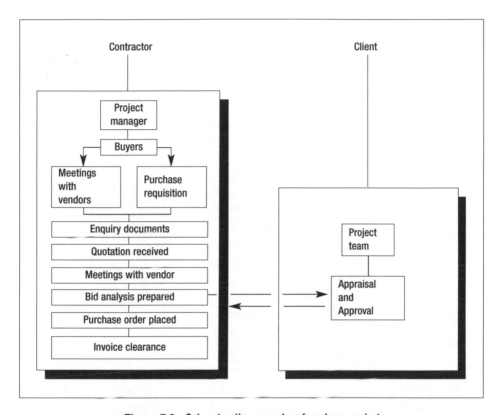

Figure 7.2 Subcontracting procedure for a large project
This diagram illustrates the respective roles of the project manager and client at the time of bidding.
Source: Adapted from Stallworthy and Kharbanda (1983)

of view between the parties. This should not be seen as an attempt by the buyer to squeeze more concessions out of a supplier who has already put in its final price. Given the timescale, bidders have to concentrate their effort on specification, price and completion date. Selection of a subcontractor can be made on this basis, but buyers will still want to hammer out the commercial terms and technical people may still want to tinker with the design.

Delay in finalizing contract terms or specification details leads to the use of letters of intent. These simply say 'we intend to place the contract with you' and in English law they are not binding on either party (see Chapter 5). Consequently, they may not have the desired effect of enabling work to start unless the contractor is able to trust the purchaser. An unconditional letter of acceptance, on the other hand, sets up a binding contract between the parties. Somewhere between the two is the instruction to proceed which authorizes the contractor to start work on specified parts of the contract and possibly states an upper limit to

									Requisition no.		
Vendors asked	(1)	(2)	(3)	(4)	(5)	(6)	Budget	All costs are tabulated in the currency indicated in the job procedure, namely			
									Selected vendor		
Exchange rate used											
(Date)									Reasons		

Questionnaire on selected vendor

- Is past record satisfactory?
- If no past record has shop been surveyed or investigated?
- Are shop facilities adequate?
- Is experience adequate?
- Is test equipment adequate?
- Are subcontractors or subvendors involved?
- If so is abnormal expediting/inspection effort required?
- Are extra exped/inspection costs expected due to shop location performance or sub-contracting?
- Do prices represent a good deal under present market conditions?

Questionnaire on selected vendor

Is past record satisfactory?	
If no past record has shop been surveyed or investigated?	
Are shop facilities adequate?	
Is experience adequate?	
Is test equipment adequate?	
Are subcontractors or subvendors involved?	
If so is abnormal expediting/ inspection effort required?	
Are extra exped/inspection costs expected due to shop location performance or sub-contracting?	
Do prices represent a good deal under present market conditions?	

Escalation ⎫
Duties ⎬ Percentage included in above price calculations
Taxes ⎭

Total percentage applied to quoted prices
Freight, packing, handling etc. amount
Total price delivered site
Estimated extras

Above normal procurement cost
Total comparative cost for selection
Quoted delivery time — Schedule:
Estimated delivery on site (including shipping time & slippage)

	Compiled by	Signature	Date
Procurement recommendation			
Technical review & recommendation			
Project approval			
Construction approval			
Management approval			
Client approval			

Figure 7.3   Example of a bid analysis form
This form is designed to make sure that all the relevant aspects of vendor selection are reviewed and compares the bid and tender price with the cost in the budget or control estimate.
Source: Adapted from Stallworthy and Kharbanda (1983)

the expenditure which the contractor can make on the authority of the letter. Purchasers usually follow up or accompany the letter of acceptance with an official order form, in order to get the contract into normal administrative and accounting procedures.

PURCHASED MATERIALS AND EQUIPMENT

Projects vary enormously in size, complexity, duration and the nature of their location (a factory in Russia, a hospital in the Middle East, a bridge over the Bristol Channel, a tunnel joining two islands). Some are less innovative and more routine than others but most require the procurement of materials and equipment such as pipe, valves and cables, none of which was designed specially for the project and the acquisition of which falls more into line with routine purchasing. All must be available on time. All must meet specification. All must be suitably priced if the project costs are to stay within budget.

Even in large projects such purchases may be handled in the purchasing department by staff not attached to the project, but who make such purchases as part of their normal work. (It may be better to second such staff to the project team if the work involved occupies them full time for significant periods.) Getting deliveries in on time, product guarantees and fixed prices, together with the legal, commercial and financial complications of operating on a world scale, can provide a variety of challenges to the purchasing staff affected.

PRICE ANALYSIS AND COST ANALYSIS

In the consideration of quotations, some form of price analysis is always used. Sometimes a more specialized technique is brought into play to support, for example, negotiations about cost-based pricing. This technique is cost analysis.

Price analysis attempts, without delving into cost details, to determine if the price offered is appropriate. It may be compared with other price offers, with prices previously paid, with the going rate (if applicable) and with the prices charged for alternatives which could be substituted for what is offered. Expert buyers deal with prices daily and, like their opposite numbers on the other side of the counter, they acquire a ready knowledge of what is appropriate. When considering something like a building contract, which does not come up daily, they refer back to prices recently quoted for comparable buildings. When several quotations are received, some will be above the average and some below it. Any prices well below the norm should be examined with care. If a supplier is short of work, a price may be quoted which covers direct labour and materials cost without making the normal contribution to overheads and profit. Accepting such an offer can be beneficial to both supplier and purchaser, but it may be prudent to ask why the supplier is short of work. It can happen to anyone, of course, but in this instance have customers been 'voting with their feet' because the supplier's work is not satisfactory?

Low prices may be the result of a totally different position: a seller may have enough work on hand to cover overheads (that is, expected sales revenue already exceeds break-even point), and is consequently able to make a profit on any price which is above direct cost. Such offers are not necessarily repeatable; next time round the price quoted may be higher to cover full costs.

Low prices may also be quoted as special introductory offers to attract new customers, giving them in effect a fair trial of the goods or services. This can be regarded as a form of compensation to the purchaser for the risk which it incurs in switching to an untried source. Some buyers do not like accepting such offers, regarding the arrangement as opportunism. Building long-term working relationships with proven suppliers matters, of course, more than a single purchase at a cheap price, but this does not exclude acceptance of special offers in all cases. Management may be pleased with the immediate cost reduction resulting from a one-off low price purchase, but there is a danger that they will expect the buyer to do even better next time. This problem can be overcome if it is made clear that special offers are, as their name implies, special to the particular occasion: they cannot be made the basis for standard price expectations.

Low prices can also be quoted simply through a mistake of the supplier or through its incompetence. Suppliers should be given the opportunity to correct such mistakes or withdraw their offers if the price appears to be suspiciously low (say more than 25 per cent below the price which would normally have been expected). Insistence on a contract at low quoted prices has led to bankrupt suppliers and unfinished contracts, and thus to additional costs for the purchaser, when this point has been ignored.

High prices may be quoted as a polite alternative to refusing to make any offer by sellers with full order books. Buyers should not write off such suppliers as too expensive since next time round they could well submit the lowest bid if conditions have changed. High prices may also be quoted because a better specification, more service, prompter delivery, etc. is offered. Obviously such offers should be considered with care. The best buy, not the cheapest price, is the buyer's objective.

Cost analysis examines prices in quite a different way from price analysis. It concentrates only on one aspect, namely how the quoted price relates to the cost of production. When large sums are involved, and a considerable amount of cost analysis needs to be done, full-time estimating staff or cost analysts may be employed for the purpose by the purchase department. These people are as well qualified to estimate a purchase price as their opposite numbers in suppliers' sales departments are to estimate a selling price: they have the same qualifications, engineering experience and costing knowledge plus specialist knowledge of sheet metal processing, light fabrication, electronics or whatever is relevant. Usually suppliers are asked to include detailed cost breakdowns with their price quotations. Some are reluctant to comply, but if one supplier does, others find it hard not to follow suit. Differences between a supplier's cost breakdown and the purchaser's cost analysis can then be examined one by one to arrive at a mutually agreed figure. Cost analysis is also used by purchasing management to set negotiating targets for buyers.

Cost analysis is a useful technique for keeping prices realistic in the absence of effective competition. It concentrates attention on what costs ought to be incurred before the work is done, instead of looking at what costs were actually incurred after the work is completed. This seems more likely to keep costs down (as well as less expensive to operate) than the alternative of wading through a supplier's accounting records after contract completion, probably employing professional auditors to do it.

AMENDMENTS TO PURCHASE ORDERS

It is sometimes unfortunately necessary to amend or even cancel purchase orders. This should, of course, be avoided if possible. Good practice is for buyer and seller to agree on all details of specification, price, terms and delivery when the order is placed, and for both parties to comply with the agreement as it affects them. Buyers do not always seem to be aware that if their purchase order constitutes a contract, they have no legal right to amend or cancel it without the seller's consent, since a contract is equally binding on both parties. In the interests of goodwill, however, suppliers are usually willing to accept amendments. Changes to specification, programme changes, increases or reductions in the quantity required, and changes from the buyer's own customers are reasons why buyers may seek to amend purchase orders.

Any amendment incurs the risk of delay and confusion. To avoid confusion it is necessary to ensure that an amendment is notified not only to the seller, but also to each internal department that received copies of the original order. One way to do this is to give details of the amendment on the same form as is used for purchase orders. If the original purchase order was numbered 7300, for example, the amendment form could be numbered 7300A. Some firms prefer to use a specially printed form. This should have the same number of copies as the purchase order form and should be distributed in the same way. Even if these methods are not used and the amendment is notified to the supplier by letter, it is important to ensure that every person who received one or more copies of the original purchase order also receives copies of all subsequent amendment letters, and files these with the order copies.

115

ELECTRONIC DATA INTERCHANGE (EDI)

Increasingly, routine communications between trading partners, such as orders, delivery schedules and invoices, go direct from computer to computer, rather than by typed documents sent by post which may then have to be typed yet again into a computer. EDI has been defined by the International Data Exchange Association as:

> the transfer of structured data, by agreed message standards, from one computer system to another, by electronic means.

A considerable saving in paperwork, postage and administrative time is claimed for EDI. Further savings may result from shorter lead times, making possible lower stocks. Against this, fees have to be charged for access to networks, annual subscriptions paid, and hardware and software bought and maintained. EDIFACT (Electronic data interchange for administration, commerce and transport) is being developed as a general message standard. Specialized standards include EDICON (electronic data interchange construction), devised by the construction industry to cover electronic trading in the industry from design, quotation and tendering through to invoicing.

Items such as request for quotation, the quotation itself, purchase order, acknowledgement, delivery instructions, dispatch note, invoice, statement and credit note are often sent electronically rather than through what is sometimes referred to as snail mail. Technical data such as specifications, CAD/CAM data, and so on, are also increasingly sent by e-mail with attachments, file transfer protocol, etc. Paperless trading systems of this kind are widely used in retailing and manufacturing and play an increasing part in project purchasing.

REFERENCES AND FURTHER READING

Baily, P. (1987), *Purchasing and Supply Management*, 5th edition, Chapman & Hall, London.
Baily, P., Farmer, D. H., Jessop, D. and Jones, D. (1998), *Purchasing Principles and Management*, 8th edition, Financial Times/Pitman Publishing, London.
Stallworthy, E. A. and Kharbanda, O. P. (1983), *Total Project Management*, Gower, Aldershot.

8 Bidding

Stephen Simister

The previous chapters of this book focused on the contractual issues more from the client's perspective. This chapter is concerned with the process suppliers of goods and services will typically go through when they are asked to submit a price for undertaking a piece of work. In order for a project to be undertaken goods and services must be procured by the client organization. Just as the client will have a strategy for procuring these goods and services, the supplier will have a similar strategy to win a particular contract.

Suppliers are not simply passive players waiting for clients to contact them. They are actively involved in creating opportunities and develop quite complex procedures to obtain the more lucrative contracts. In this chapter we examine the entire bid process from when a supplier is first considered for a particular piece of work to when contracts are signed between the client and the supplier.

MANAGING THE BID PROCESS

If companies are not successful in submitting winning bids their workload will soon dry up. Therefore considerable attention is required to manage the bid process. It is common for a proposal manager to oversee the entire process. The proposal manager is the project manager for the bid process. He or she should treat the bid process like a project and plan and manage it like any project. The proposal manager will require support from a number of people including account managers who may have particular knowledge of the client and technical managers with detailed knowledge of the tasks to be undertaken during the potential implementation of the project. In larger organizations there may be a business development manager who is often an experienced project manager in his or her own right and is now using that experience to win more work for the company. The people required to support the proposal manager can be identified in a responsibility chart.

The bid process is managed as a single entity within the bidding organization but the activities that take place are often delegated to separate units within it. The reason for this is that the process, while seeming superficially quite simple, is actually complex. Bidding for a piece of work represents a considerable amount of investment for an organization and with a typical success rate of 1 in 5 there is constant pressure to improve this ratio and keep the costs of bidding as low as possible. As shown in the flow chart in Figure 8.1, the bid process has three stages which will now be considered in more detail.

THE BID PROCESS

The bid process is the process that the supplier will undertake in order to arrive

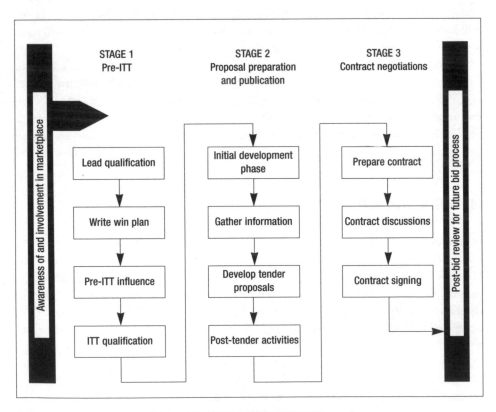

Figure 8.1   Main activities in the bid process

at a successful bid which secures a contract with the client. It contains activities which start as soon as a lead has been detected, continue with the response to the invitation to tender (ITT) and finish after winning or losing the opportunity. The process can be divided into three stages:

Stage 1: Pre-ITT Suppliers try to influence the client or organization writing the ITT and to define their strategy after reception of the ITT. The goal in this stage is to establish yourself as the proactive bidder in the client's mind and where possible influence the writing of the ITT so it fits your company's profile the most appropriately. This could be where your company has access to a particular technology or skill that is not widely available elsewhere.

Stage 2: Proposal preparation and publication The supplier creates a proposal which is 100 per cent compliant with the ITT, develops a proposal presentation and executes the post-tender submission strategy defined in the win plan. The goal of these activities is to become the preferred supplier.

Stage 3: Contract negotiations An implementation agreement is reached with the most favourable terms and conditions for the supplier. The ultimate goal of this phase is a contract for the implementation of the client's requirements.

Some of the activities that need to take place within these three stages are shown in the flow chart in Figure 8.1 and are discussed below.

STAGE 1: PRE-ITT

This stage is concerned with actually getting on the bidding list that a client is putting together. Clients will typically select only a few firms, perhaps three to five, to submit bids for their project. One of the initial difficulties clients face is how to pick the suppliers that will be invited to bid.

Lead qualification

To be invited to submit a pre-qualification ITT the supplier must be active in the marketplace. This will typically involve not only undertaking work in a particular business activity, but also ensuring that personnel are involved in business development with current and potential future clients. Whilst most organizations will have about two-thirds of their business as repeat work, they are constantly losing clients for a variety of reasons and have to seek out new opportunities. It is during this phase that a decision must be made as to whether a bid will be submitted. It may happen that whilst a bid sounded attractive in its outline form, the pre-qualification documentation may show that the project is not suited to the supplier. Typical areas that suppliers will need to consider in this respect are shown in Figure 8.2.

Once a decision has been made to submit a pre-qualification bid a strategy will need to be developed to submit a winning bid.

Write win plan

The areas that need consideration to decide if the supplier should bid or not are essentially the ones that also need considering in writing a bid plan. The supplier needs to put itself in the client's position and ask why it should be given the work. A lot of suppliers use a SWOT (Strengths, Weaknesses, Opportunities, Threats) analysis in this respect. The supplier has made a positive decision to bid for the work and will commit resources to this bid. If unsuccessful, the supplier should be able to identify some benefit of having undertaken the bid and this also needs to form part of the win plan.

For our organization:

- Do we have the resources available to prepare the tender?
- Do we have the resources available to undertake the project if we win the work?
- How strong is the competition?
- Do we have a solution to offer the client?
- Does the project offer us the business opportunity in which we are interested?
- What standards do we have to comply with?
- Are we strong in this area or is it an area we wish to develop?
- What are our potential contractual obligations and can we fulfil them?

For our subcontractor suppliers:

- What is their position in relation to this project?
- Do they have a solution?
- Are they known to be favoured by the client?

For the client:

- Does the client have a budget and do we know what it is?
- Has the client clearly articulated what it wants?
- In the client organization who is for and against us and what is their relationship with the project?
- Has the client undertaken a similar venture before and who with?

Figure 8.2   Typical questions considered in decision to tender at the pre-qualification stage

Pre-ITT influence

Whilst developing the pre-qualification bid, the supplier is normally allowed direct contact with the client organization. This opportunity should be used to maximum effect. The supplier should be asking pertinent questions that demonstrate its expertise in the area of interest. In some instances, it may be possible to suggest to the client that a supplier's technology is the only one to use and try to gain an advantage over other technology.

During the client meetings, it should also be possible to determine who are the key decision-makers in the organization and which of these are for or against the supplier. Effort can then be directed towards trying to win over the latter people whilst supporting those who favour the supplier.

ITT qualification

The pre-qualification bid has been submitted and the supplier has been successful in going forward to the next stage. The supplier needs to reflect on its performance for further bid opportunities as well as prepare itself for moving into the next stage.

If a supplier is unsuccessful at pre-qualifying, most clients are willing to provide a debriefing session which allows the supplier the opportunity to find out what went wrong, which areas it needs to work on and, for future market intelligence, who won through to the next stage.

STAGE 2: PROPOSAL PREPARATION AND PUBLICATION

This stage is concerned with putting together tender documents which not only comply with the client's requirements, but also demonstrate the supplier's competence in the tendering process. The tendering process is quite an investment in resource typically adding some 5 per cent to the cost of most contracts.

Initial development phase

The pre-qualification document will form the basis of the tender and act as a structure on which to build. The first task is to check that all the tender documentation has been received and that the supplier understands what needs to be delivered. It may be that the scope of work has been changed since the qualification stage and this needs to be studied to ensure that the supplier is still interested in submitting a bid.

Gather information

Once the requirement is understood, an appropriate solution can be developed. Information to develop the solution needs to be gathered and, if required, expertise outside the organization sought. The information gathering exercise is crucial as it generally takes some time and whilst it is still ongoing people have to make decisions based on what is currently available.

Develop tender proposals

This is where the bulk of the work lies. The supplier has to develop its proposals to a stage where it is confident that they meet the client requirements and in such detail that accurate cost and programme estimates can be made. The amount of detail involved is generally not far short of what is required to actually execute the project. Once again, the supplier will generally be liaising with the client, trying to find out if there are any preferred solutions and obtaining feedback on suggestions being put forward.

Post-tender activities

After the tender has been submitted, the supplier will generally be invited to discuss its proposals with the client, once the client has had time to analyse them. Normally the client will wish to clarify various aspects of the tender and investigate if there is any room for negotiation over aspects of the proposal.

STAGE 3: CONTRACT NEGOTIATIONS

Once the tender has been accepted, a formal contract needs to be drawn up which sets out the obligations of the supplier and client in the execution of the project. While the outline of the contract will have formed part of the tender documentation, the exact details are often subject to negotiation after the tender has been awarded. For instance, the exact starting date of the project will need to be set.

Prepare contract

A contract that reflects the type of relationship the two parties want to enter into needs to be drafted. Some industries, such as construction and building, have a wide range of standard forms of contract (see Chapter 4). Alternatively, clients may have their own standard forms. In all circumstances, a contract has to be drawn up which states the intentions of the parties and accurately reflects both the client's requirements and the supplier's tender. During this phase, the supplier also needs to think about what its stance will be during the contract discussions. There may be a particular point which is important to the supplier and to get agreement on this it will be willing to sacrifice some other detail. These items need thinking about so that the personnel undertaking the negotiations know what approach to take on crucial issues.

Contract discussions

This is where the finite detail of the client–supplier relationship is dealt with. Both sides have invested considerable resources to reach this negotiation stage. However, both sides also want to try to negotiate the most favourable conditions for themselves. In construction it is not uncommon for contractors to commence building on-site whilst still negotiating the details of the contract. This is obviously not a desirable situation and the contract should be signed prior to any work commencing on the project. Ultimately both parties have to sign the document and so there must be agreement on the terms and conditions set out in the contract.

Contract signing

The actual act of signing can in some circumstances be rather a show-piece with the press invited to a ceremonial signing of the contract. In most circumstances, the signing of the contract is undertaken by management, typically at board level. These people will normally have not been involved in the negotiation of the contract so will be trusting that their negotiating staff have done an appropriate job.

POST-BID REVIEW

Once the contract has been signed, the supplier then concentrates on actually delivering the goods and services that the client requires. As part of the bidding process a review of the bid should be undertaken to identify lessons learned for use in the next exercise. Topics to be addressed might include the following:

1. Why did the client choose our company?
2. Was the client completely satisfied with our presentation and proposals?
3. Was our approach the right one or just the best of a bad bunch?
4. Was the offered solution correct or did protracted negotiations have to take place to hone the requirements?
5. Were our cost and programme appropriate to meet the client's needs?

While the bid process should be evaluated immediately after the successful signing of the contract, it may also be useful to hold a review once the project is complete. A post-project review can provide an insight as to the accuracy of the tender put forward measured against the executed costs. This can provide input into future tenders and adjustments made to future bids accordingly.

CONCLUSIONS

For suppliers the bidding process consists of three stages:

1. Pre-ITT.
2. Proposal preparation and publication.
3. Contract negotiations.

While the supplier's aim is to win the contract, it does not want to do so at any price. The supplier has to be able to influence the client to the extent that the client wants the supplier to win the contract as well. In these circumstances, the supplier will be able to negotiate quite favourable terms for itself.

Bidding is concerned with predicting the future since the supplier has to commit to a price and time framework before the work is undertaken. Because of this the supplier has to build up an accurate database of information drawn from previous contracts and evaluated against the bids for those contracts. The post-bid review is vital in assisting this feedback.

Suppliers have to become experts in preparing and submitting winning bids if they are to survive and grow in an increasingly competitive market.

REFERENCES AND FURTHER READING

Bartholomew, S. H. (1999), *Estimating and Bidding for Heavy Construction*, Prentice-Hall, San Francisco, CA.

Bernink, B. (1995), 'Winning contracts', in J. R. Turner (ed.), *The Commercial Project Manager*, McGraw-Hill, London.

Miles, M. (1992), *Stronger Competitive Bidding*, Lawrence & Leong Publishing, New York.

9 Managing variations, claims and disputes

Peter Marsh

Like all good relationships, contracts can go wrong. Often we would like to pretend otherwise, to stick our heads in the sand and assume all is and will remain rosy. Usually it will be so, but we must make plans for things going wrong. Most contracts have written into them clauses to deal with the unusual, and that is right and proper. If variations and other disputes are planned for, then their impact and cost will be reduced.

In this chapter we consider how to deal with unplanned or unusual events. We start with variations. Variations are inevitable; we cannot predict the future and plan for every eventuality. Hopefully they can be kept to a minimum, and variations arising from poor quality of design and decision-making avoided; variations will be essential rather than nice-to-have changes or plain mistakes. Many variations will result in a claim for additional payment. Some claims will be accepted, some challenged. If the parties cannot agree a claim, they will go into dispute, and that then needs to be resolved. We consider the impact of the Construction Act 1998 and the Arbitration Act 1996, both of which arose partially out of the Latham Report (1994), and we consider the response of contracting practice to them. Finally, we describe adjudication procedures.

VARIATIONS

Variations may be described not unfairly as the cancer of contracting. Their cumulative effect can combine to destroy the best of contracts; the habit of ordering them is in itself a disease. What causes this disease? The causes are many but the principal ones are as follows:

1. *Inadequate allowance for thinking time*   It is distressing but true that many managers are not convinced that progress is being made unless holes are

125

being dug, equipment is being manufactured or code written, and so start work before the project is properly planned. Morris and Hough (1987) describe how the project manager on the computerization of PAYE resisted starting before he was ready, and the project had a successful outcome; whereas Hougham (1996) describes how, ten years later, the team working on the computerization of London Ambulance started work before they were ready, leading to a national disaster.

2. *Inadequate specifications*   One finds a great reluctance amongst people to be completely specific as to what they require, as to the services to be provided by the purchaser and as to the actual conditions under which the work will be carried out.

3. *Insufficient attention as to whether what the tenderer is offering is exactly what the purchaser wants to buy*   The tendency is to say 'It seems generally all right; we can sort out the detail later'.

4. *Lack of discipline*   In the matter of variations it is often far easier to say 'Yes, while we are about it we might as well have that done', than to say firmly 'No, it's not necessary'.

5. *Improvements to avoid obsolescence*   With the rapid rate of technical change taking place today, any major plant or system is likely to be out of date in some respects long before it is completed. This applies particularly to information technology and telecommunications systems. It may well be that some upgrading is essential now but it is often far better to have the system built and installed as it was originally designed and ensure that the facilities exist for later developments. The later the stage in the project, the more it costs to make changes (Turner 1999), and so you reach a point where changes must be avoided unless they are absolute show-stoppers.

6. *Genuinely unforeseeable circumstances*   It would be idle to pretend that no variation is ever justified. There are times when it is essential to vary the works or system. Variations must be allowed for in the original thinking and procedures set in place for their control. Anyone who thinks they can avoid variations completely is a fool or a liar, or both. Therefore variations must be accepted and planned for.

It is often not appreciated that even a quite simple change of specification can have a dramatic impact on a contractor, especially if that contractor also has a design responsibility. The change may involve the contractor in:

- design work which because of the change is now not needed;
- additional design work including studying the consequential effect of the variation on a number of drawings;
- cancellation of, or modification to, orders already placed on their own works or outside suppliers;

- the placing of new orders;
- delay and/or re-phasing of the design and manufacturing programme to accommodate the variation;
- delay in delivery of material due to re-phasing of work or concentration of work into a shorter period with consequential overtime costs and loss of productivity;
- extending the period of the contract.

Figure 9.1 illustrates how these items contribute to the cost of a variation. It follows from this data that the cost effect of the variation will be reduced the earlier it is ordered. The figure takes no account of the effect of the variation on the programme as a whole. If it is small, a single variation will have little impact on the programme (though the new engineering contract says that all variations must be assumed to have a time and cost impact, (ICE 1995)). The figure also takes no account of the double administrative cost effect on the contractor of having to go through the same operation twice. Again, if it is only one item, few contractors would seriously quarrel with accepting it as one of the hazards of contracting.

The trouble starts when not one variation but a whole series of variations causes a disruption to the regular progress of the work, loss of productivity and a substantial extension to the contract programme. The time spent by the

Additions	Deductions
1. Works or bought-out cost of the new item	1. Works or bought-out cost of the item to be replaced
2. Percentage for overheads and profit related to works or bought-out cost	2. Percentage for overheads and profit related to works or bought-out cost
3. Man-hours cost for the installation of the new item	3. Man-hours cost for the installation of the item to be replaced
4. Percentage for overheads and profit on installation costs	4. Percentage for overheads and profit on installation costs
5. Charge for additional design including overheads and profit necessary to incorporate the new item	5. Charge for any design work including overheads and profit which will no longer be required
6. Design, labour and material costs, related overheads and profit and consequential modification to the remainder of the plant system including study of the drawings to see if any are necessary	
7. Cancellation charges payable to outside suppliers	

Figure 9.1   Factors affecting the cost of a variation
In this example one or more items of equipment are to be deleted from the specification and replaced by others

contractor's head office staff will then become totally disproportionate to that anticipated at tender, and coupled with the extension to the programme may affect the contractor's ability to undertake other work. Under these circumstances, the purchaser must expect that the contractor will seek to recover these additional costs and also seek recompense for the impact on its ability to obtain other business.

Claims for delay and disruption are never easy although those for site work where the facts can often be established from contemporary site records are easier than those for overheads. However, it is important to distinguish between the two bases of claim which the contractor may make for head office overheads and profit. First, there is a claim for overheads only which is based on the additional managerial time and expense required to deal with the problems created by the excessive number of variations. To establish such a claim the contractor must provide evidence of the additional managerial time expended and not simply add on an arbitrary percentage (see the case of *Tate and Lyle* v. *GLC* (1982)).

The claim for overheads and profit is for the allegation that by reason of the extended contract period and involvement of their staff, the contractor has been deprived of the opportunity to earn a contribution to its fixed overheads and profit. In the building industry, it is common for the contractor to calculate such a claim by the use of a formula. However, in principle that must be wrong. The formula is only a means of quantification. Before it can be used, the contractor must prove that as a result of the delay, they suffered some loss by showing that the delayed contract deprived them of the opportunity to obtain other work on which a margin for overheads and profit could have been earned. This means that the contractor must prove:

- there was other work available which would have been profitable;
- that they did not obtain this work; and
- that the failure to obtain the work was the direct result of the delayed contract.

It is only when these facts have been proved that the use of a formula as a method of quantification of loss has any validity. The difficulties of proving those facts are recognized. However, the basic principle of English law is that it is for the contractor to prove it has suffered a loss arising directly from the purchaser's actions, and the automatic substitution of a formula which takes no account of actual loss suffered cannot be justified.

PRICING OF VARIATIONS

There are often difficulties in negotiating variations, especially on lump sum contracts where there may be no mechanism for doing so established in the contract itself. The purchaser will think the contractor is taking them for a ride, but may genuinely be unappreciative of what trouble and cost their simple instruction has caused. The purchaser will also be acutely aware that it is impractical for them to get competitive quotations. The contractor may be anxious to recover any ground lost in post-tender negotiations. Neither side is likely to be in a mood for making concessions but the purchaser is likely to be in the weaker negotiating position.

For contracts priced on a bill of quantities or schedule of rates (see Chapter 2), the problem is not as great provided that the quantities in the bill are not grossly exceeded or diminished as a result of the variation and the work is being executed under the same conditions. Different conditions may, for instance, be work conducted at a different time of the year than it was anticipated that the original work would be executed.

With lump sum contracts for which there are no rates quoted for individual items of work the problem is more difficult. In the new engineering contract (ICE 1995), a valiant effort has been made to solve this problem by requiring the contractor to quote as part of their tender a schedule of cost components. For the purpose of tender comparison quantities are assumed by the employer and included in the invitation to tender.

This schedule gives the cost components in terms of various categories of labour for design, manufacturing and site work together with related overhead percentages, the costs of materials and plant and other overhead costs. The variation is then priced by making a comparison between the forecast actual cost for the work originally included in the tender and the forecast actual cost arising as a result of the variation together with the contractor's fee. The comparison is specifically not made by deleting the original contract price for the work and substituting the forecast actual cost. It is also made clear that the variation is not to be priced by using any of the rates and prices included in the contract, say, in the bill of quantities.

There are several difficulties with this method apart from its obvious administrative cost and complexity. One is that while one can compare staff and labour rates, and indeed overheads on their own, they mean very little without knowledge of the contractor's productivity. One firm's rates may be higher than another's but this may well be offset by higher efficiency.

TIMING OF PRICE NEGOTIATIONS

A vital factor in the successful control of variation is the timing of price negotiations. Too often because of the pressure for the achievement of physical progress of the work and the complexities in the price change, instructions are given to the contractor to make the change, with the alteration in price to be negotiated later. Ideally the sequence of events should be as follows:

1. The purchaser decides that a particular variation would be desirable.
2. The contractor is instructed to assess the effect of the proposed variation in terms of:
   - price
   - time
   - performance.
3. The contractor submits their proposals under these headings.
4. If the purchaser decides to proceed with the variation, then they negotiate with the contractor on the amendments to the price, time for completion and performance requirements.
5. Once agreement has been reached, the purchaser issues a formal variation order in standard form serially numbered.
6. The contractor proceeds with work.

The new engineering contract uses a similar series of steps. It seems a long series and the temptation is to go straight ahead and tell the contractor to start work. Indeed there will be genuine emergencies when it is necessary to do just that and tidy up the paperwork afterwards. But in so doing, not only any possible negotiating advantage is lost, but also any enthusiasm on the part of the purchaser's staff to make variations is removed and financial control of the contract is lost. Except in the case of a real emergency it should be difficult to order variations.

CLAIMS

Claims can be considered under three headings:

- ex gratia
- from excessive ordering of variations
- default by the client in their obligations under the contract.

EX-GRATIA CLAIMS

These are claims made when the contractor can find no contractual basis for the claim but considers that because of some unexpected event there is a moral or commercial obligation on the client to pay compensation. An example would be a fixed price contract entered into before the huge and unexpected rise in oil prices in the 1970s which could not have been foreseen by the contractor and for which therefore no allowance was made in its price. The difficulty for the contractor is that while it may be true that they suffered losses, there is ordinarily no reason why the client should pay compensation. Payment can only possibly be justified if, in the face of serious and unforeseeable difficulties in the performance of the contract, for which the contract provides no right for additional payment, the contractor made extraordinary efforts to overcome these and completed the work to specification and by the time for completion. Then the contractor may rely on the client's goodwill but on nothing else. Faced with a contractor going bankrupt or completing, it may be cheaper for a client to make an ex-gratia payment.

CLAIMS ARISING OUT OF EXCESSIVE VARIATIONS

These have been discussed above under the heading 'Variations'.

CLAIMS ARISING OUT OF THE CLIENT'S DEFAULT

Under all contracts there are some obligations for the client to perform, for instance in making the site available and supplying information and facilities which if they are not provided on time and to specification will result in the contractor incurring additional costs. A claim for the recovery of those costs is often linked with one relating to the number of variations. The great difficulty for the contractor is that although it may be obvious that work has been disrupted and delayed, it may also be very difficult to itemize each cause to a specific effect and therefore to additional cost.

It may be possible today for the contractor by the use of an appropriate computer program to use the technique of impact analysis. This establishes the impact of individual causes on a series of logically connected events within the network for the contract. However, the practical application technique requires the knowledge of how the work was programmed, how it progressed, when the delaying events occurred and the interaction between one delay and another. This emphasizes the need for contemporary data and for the work on the analysis to start at the time and not at the end of the contract.

Because of the difficulties of determining the effect of individual events contractors often try to present their claim on a 'total loss', 'global' or 'rolled up' basis. This has the obvious advantage that the contractor does not have to prove the individual loss arising from each event, but only make a broad-brush calculation based on the total cost overrun. From the employer's point of view, the

131

disadvantage is that they do not have particulars of the sums being claimed. Nor do they have the basis on which it is alleged in each instance that they, rather than the contractor, or some external cause, is responsible for the loss in question. The employer's ability to challenge the contractor's claim is therefore much reduced.

From the decisions in English law on the validity of 'rolled up claims', the position is that the contractor must demonstrate that they have made every effort practicable to itemize the causes of delay or disruption and their individual effects. Only where the contractor can show that the complexity of the interrelationship between a number of causes is such that it is impractical to do this is it likely that a court or arbitrator would accept a 'rolled up claim'.

CLAIMS PRESENTATION AND MANAGEMENT

There are a few basic rules to be followed in preparing for and presenting claims:

1. Consider the possible areas of claim from the start of the contract and plan accordingly. Don't wait until they happen.
2. Make sure that all involved know any particular areas of risk which have been accepted under the contract which might normally entitle a claim to be made but would not on this contract.
3. Keep accurate and contemporary records from the start of the contract. A good factual site diary prepared at the time is essential on a construction contract. (The problem is that this does lead to the impression that the first file opened by a contractor on a construction site is the claims file. Unfortunately, it is necessary. However, ensure that it is understood that the purpose of the file is to resolve problems, not make claims.)
4. Where it is considered that a claim may arise in respect of design work, ensure that the records are sufficiently detailed to identify the number of man-hours spent and by whom on the revisions to each drawing or the preparation of new revised drawings, and the reasons for the revisions.
5. Make a record of the requirements for the giving of notice of claims under the contract and ensure that these are followed through in practice.
6. Ensure that all correspondence with and from the client which could have an impact on claims is reviewed as are all minutes of meetings.
7. In presenting the claim make sure that it contains:
   - a short executive summary;
   - clear references to the terms of contract on which the claim is based;
   - all essential data which is required to understand the claim, such as critical dates, extensions of time applied for and granted, variation orders issued, etc.;

...me, minutes and other documents supportive of the

...hanges occurred in the ways in which disputes under a
...i, especially if the contract falls within the definition of a
...under the Housing Grants Construction and Regeneration
...iction Act). First, was the Arbitration Act 1996 and, second,
...sions of the Construction Act relating to the determination of
...cation.

ACT 1996

... had gained a bad reputation for being too slow, too expensive and too
. with technical issues having no substantive merit. The primary reasons
₃ are listed below:

...n practice arbitration procedures had closely followed those of the courts
although not required to do so by law. Arbitration had been referred to as
'wigless' litigation and borrowings from court procedures included such
elements as discovery of documents and the rules of evidence.

● There had been in many instances no power to exclude in advance of the
arbitration proceedings through the commercial contract itself the right to
appeal to the High Court on a point of law.

● Clauses were invalid that allowed an arbitrator to decide with the agreement
of the parties on the grounds of equity and fairness *ex aequo et bono*.

● English arbitration law was difficult to discover being contained in the
judgements of the courts and the two principal statutes, the Arbitration Acts
of 1950 and 1979.

For all these and other reasons it was decided that a new Act was required to set
out in a form which was comprehensive and easy to read the English law relating
to arbitration. The following changes were introduced by the Act:

1. The introduction of an objectives clause which states:
   ● the object of arbitration is to obtain the fair resolution of disputes by an
   impartial tribunal without unnecessary expense and delay; and
   ● the parties should be free to agree how their disputes should be resolved
   subject only to such safeguards as are necessary in the public interest.

133

2. The tribunal has the power to decide on all procedural and evidential matters subject only to the right of the parties to decide such matters for themselves. These include:

   - whether any and if so which documents or classes of documents should be disclosed;
   - whether any and if so what questions should be put and answered by the parties and when and in what form this should be done;
   - whether to apply strict rules of evidence or any other rules as to admissibility, relevance or weight of any material;
   - whether and to what extent the tribunal should itself take the initiative in ascertaining the facts and the law;
   - whether and to what extent there should be written or oral evidence or submissions.

Hence the conduct of the arbitration proceedings, provided that the parties agree, or in the absence of their agreement the tribunal decides, can be tailored in such a way as to achieve the objectives of the Act.

On the subject of appeals, it is now open to the parties to agree in their commercial contract to exclude the right of appeal entirely. In any event, an appeal can only be made if:

- the parties agree; or
- the court decides that the decision of the tribunal was obviously wrong; or
- the question is one of general public importance and the decision of the tribunal is at least open to serious doubt and that it is just and proper in all the circumstances that the court should determine the question.

Unless the court decides that the decision of the tribunal was obviously wrong, it is likely that in practice it will only allow an appeal if the point of law concerns the interpretation of a standard contract in general use, and which is of significant importance to the industry concerned with that form of contract. The court is given wide powers to support the arbitration tribunal, especially in relation to complying with the tribunal's orders regarding procedural matters, such as the production of documents, exchanging witness statements, and so on, which have in the past been the cause of substantial delays.

There is one significant problem with the Act which has caused some to recommend that arbitration should not be included within a construction contract although all standard forms in general such as those issued by the ICE and the JCT do retain arbitration. In the past where an application was made to the court for summary judgement under Order 14 because it was considered there was no arguable defence to the plaintiff's claim, then even if the contract contained a clause that all disputes were to be referred to arbitration, the court had a discretion to hear the application instead of staying it to arbitration.

Under section 9 of the new Act the discretion of the court has now been removed, and it appears that if the contract does contain an arbitration clause, then the court must stay the matter to arbitration. This has been confirmed in the case of *Halki Shipping Corporation* v. *Sopex Oils* (1997) where there was no real defence to the claim by the plaintiff, but as there was an arbitration clause in the contract the dispute had to be stayed to arbitration.

Applications for summary judgement are relatively common in the construction industry usually for payment for work done for which a certificate of the architect or engineer has been issued but payment has not been made. Now it appears that assuming there is an arbitration clause in the contract the court would not be able to hear the application if it was disputed by the other party, however flimsy the defence.

Leaving that point aside what are the perceived advantages of arbitration as opposed to recourse to the courts?

- Confidentiality: the proceedings are in private.
- Informality.
- Speed.
- Use by the arbitrator of his or her technical knowledge.

However, apart from the first, these advantages are all dependent upon the parties agreeing as to how the proceedings should be handled or the arbitrator taking a very firm line and using to the full his or her powers under the Act. The likelihood of either party agreeing to anything except something to their own advantage, which means that it will almost certainly be to the disadvantage of the other, seems remote.

That brings out the essential point that arbitration will only ever be as good as the arbitrator, and highlights the importance of his or her selection. Good arbitrators are usually expensive and it is, of course, one of the disadvantages of arbitration that the costs of the arbitrator have to be paid for by the parties. Also, even though the courts can be slow, they are available to the parties. In arbitration, the parties' choice of the person to act as arbitrator can be affected by his or her availability to act, since good arbitrators do tend to get booked up well in advance. With the reforms currently taking place in civil procedure, the advantages of arbitration over the courts, except for the issue of privacy, do not appear to be significant.

ADJUDICATION

One of the key reforms proposed by the Latham Report (1994) was that there should be in all construction contracts a procedure for the rapid resolution of disputes. This procedure would operate while the contract was being performed with either party having the right to challenge the decision at arbitration once the contract was completed. In the event, after a long gestation period, the Construction Act provides that:

> a party to a construction contract as defined by the Act has the right to refer a dispute arising under the contract for adjudication under a procedure complying with the Act.

The Act then goes on to provide that:

> the contract shall:
>
> (a) enable a party to give notice at any time of their intention to refer a dispute to adjudication
> (b) provide a timetable with the object of securing the appointment of the adjudicator and referral of the dispute to him within 7 days of such notice
> (c) require the adjudicator to reach a decision within 28 days of referral or such longer period as is agreed by the parties after the dispute has been referred
> (d) allow the adjudicator to extend the period of 28 days by up to 14 days, with the consent of the party by whom the dispute was referred
> (e) impose upon the adjudicator to act impartially
> (f) enable the adjudicator to take the initiative in ascertaining the facts and the law.

It also provides that:

- the contract shall provide that the decision of the adjudicator is binding until the dispute is finally determined by legal proceedings, arbitration or agreement between the parties. The parties could accept the decision of the adjudicator was final
- the adjudicator is immune from being sued for anything done or not done by him in deciding the dispute unless the act or omission is in bad faith
- if the contract does not contain a procedure complying with these requirements, then the Scheme for Construction Contracts shall apply.

At the time there was significant antagonism towards these provisions, particularly from leading construction lawyers. This was based on their views that adjudication was not needed, it was not workable and would increase rather than decrease antagonism in the industry. After over a year's operation of the Act, it is clear that it is workable and it has provided quick answers to resolving disputes which would have previously dragged on for months. Much of the credit for this must be given to the judges of the Technology and Construction Court for their robust upholding of the adjudicator's decisions when challenged on legal technicalities. However, it does not seem to have reduced adversarialism which remains a chronic construction industry problem. It is clear that the JCT amendments do comply with the Act and therefore the Statutory Scheme will not apply to contracts let under any of its standard forms. With the ICE amendments, it is not so certain that they comply since the ICE has sought to retain the decision-making powers of the engineer. Its amendments state that there is no dispute between the parties until either the engineer has given his or her decision and one party objects to it or the engineer has failed to give a decision within the time allowed. Only then can a dispute be referred to adjudication. Whether this trick will work or not remains to be seen. It clearly does not comply with the spirit of the Act.

Many construction contracts are not let on these standard forms and unless they are drafted to include provisions relating to the adjudication which comply with the Act then the Statutory Scheme will be deemed to be substituted. In summary the Scheme provides for:

- the method of appointing the adjudicator;
- the adjudicator being a natural person not in the employ of either party;
- powers for the adjudicator but only with the consent of the parties to deal with related disputes under different contracts;
- the right of the adjudicator to open, review and revise any certificate except one which under the contract is final and conclusive;
- the adjudicator to act impartially and in accordance with the terms of the contract and its applicable law;
- the adjudicator to take the initiative in ascertaining the facts and the law necessary to determine the dispute and to decide on the procedure to be followed in the adjudication.

The weakest area in the Act is the lack of any clear means of enforcement of the adjudicator's decision. It appears that the only way in which enforcement is possible is by an application to the courts for summary judgement. However, there is the obvious risk that any such application might be opposed by the other party. Further, assuming that the contract contained an arbitration clause, the case would have to be stayed by the court to arbitration under the 1996 Arbitration Act and the decision in Halki Shipping Corporation to which reference was made earlier. It is for this reason that the JCT and the ICE in their amendments to their standard forms of contract have provided that the arbitration clause does not apply to any action to enforce the decision of an adjudicator.

REFERENCES AND FURTHER READING

Hougham, M. (1996), 'London Ambulance Service computer aided dispatch system', *International Journal of Project Management*, **14**(2).

Institution of Civil Engineers (ICE) (1995), *The Engineering and Construction Contract*, 2nd edition, Thomas Telford, London.

Latham, Sir Michael (1994), *Constructing the Team, Final Report of the Government/Industry Review of Procurement and Contractual Arrangements in the UK Construction Industry*, The Stationery Office, London.

Morris, P. W. G. and Hough, G. (1987), *The Anatomy of Major Projects: The Reality of Project Management*, Wiley, Chichester.

Turner, J. R. (1999), *The Handbook of Project-based Management*, 2nd edition, McGraw-Hill, London.

Index

This index is arranged in word-by-word order, e.g. 'price negotiations for contract variations' precedes 'priced contract with an activity schedule'. Titles of documents are given in italics. Headings which are initialized forms of phrases (e.g. SOR) are treated as words.

The Relationship Manager

The Next Generation of Project Management

Tony Davis and Richard Pharro

Traditionally, project managers have been allocated a project and their role has been to deliver on time, to quality standards and within budget. With hindsight the client only recognises what they really want once the project is delivered – and there is often a gap between expectation and final product. The project management role is now changing and the total impact on the business needs to be addressed more effectively – enter the Relationship Manager.

The true role of the Relationship Manager is to act as an orchestral conductor;

- to go to the client and demonstrate his understanding of the client's short-, medium- and long-term objectives;
- to translate this into a form which the project team can address;
- to receive from the project team a specification of the work to be undertaken, including plans, estimates and schedules, together with detailed work and cost breakdown structures to check that they have really understood what needs to be done and by when – and only when the Relationship Manager is satisfied does he return to the client to sell VALUE.

The Relationship Manager has been written to fill the gap between technical and business aspects of successful project delivery. It provides practical guidance on how to make this new way of working a reality and details the skills and techniques necessary to make a success of the latest developments in project management.

GOWER

The Bid Manager's Handbook

David Nickson

Winning significant business on the right terms is an increasingly complex, challenging and time-consuming task, and a successful bid is a vital part of any business offering its services or products to another. This book will help you to enhance the probability of success in winning bids at the desired margins and to set up and run effectively a bid management team. Aimed at two main groups of readers (sales staff managing multi-disciplinary bid teams, and project and technical managers who find themselves managing a bid to support a sales campaign), *The Bid Manager's Handbook* provides an invaluable resource in the battle to win new business.

Taking an extremely practical approach and using real-life examples, David Nickson leads the reader through every stage of planning for, producing and delivering a bid. By the end of the book you will:

- know what needs to be done
- know how to present the information to the prospective client effectively
- have gained the writing and editorial skills needed to put a sales case across
- have identified the skills that are needed to manage a bid.

Crucially it also shows how to save time – the most important commodity in any bid as it is always a scarce resource – without affecting quality. In short, *The Bid Manager's Handbook* is the definitive guide to managing winning bids effectively and efficiently.

GOWER

Project Management

Eighth Edition

Dennis Lock

Dennis Lock's masterly exposition of the principles and practice
of project management has been pre-eminent in its field for three
decades. It examines the entire process in detail, from initial
appraisal to final closedown, demonstrating techniques that range
from the simplest of manual charts to sophisticated computer systems.
The text is reinforced throughout with case examples and diagrams.

For this eighth edition the text has been meticulously revised and
updated, and includes a brand new chapter on aspects of managing
project risk. As with previous editions, great care has been taken to
ensure that the text style remains easy to read, with clear diagrams
and a construction that is logically organized, well indexed and
simple to navigate. The result is certain to maintain the book's
acclaimed status as the standard project management work for
managers and students alike.

Project Management is the best British textbook on the subject.
It is preferred by students for its approachable style and offers
excellent value for money.

GOWER

Project Management for Successful Product Innovation

Alan Webb

This comprehensive book provides a complete guide to managing projects involving the development of new products. It aims to give the practising project manager an insight into the many processes that are involved in handling one of the most complex of industrial activities.

The book is arranged in a logical sequence covering the development of project management, project management structures, aspects of planning, monitoring and control, economics and value management, design management, intellectual property issues and production start-up. Particular emphasis has been given to risk management which is recognized as both a difficult subject and also one of growing importance to today's project manager, especially in product innovation. A complete explanation is given of the latest and most relevant techniques together with guidance as to where and how they should be applied. Where software tools are available these are named and, in some cases, brief descriptions are included; in all cases contact details of the vendors are provided.

GOWER